Acknowledgements

If I should name everyone who has helped me in some way or other with this book, the list would be very long indeed. Many people have contributed towards this book and I thank them all. But I would particularly like to thank the many colleagues whose participation in my research and consultancy exercises brought insight and a depth of understanding to previously obscure areas. I only hope I have been able to use these insights wisely. Many 'clients' have also assisted in this process especially, but not always, themselves the survivors of child abuse.

I also wish to thank Berly Cauter and Jane Tunstill, for their interest, help and support. Special thanks to my husband Peter for all his hard work and patience. Without his help, this book would have taken much longer to complete.

Contents

Preface

Books on child protection which address both the practice and the survival of the worker are always in demand because the risks are high for all involved; the children, their families, the workers and the agency. Child abuse brings together at least six emotive topics: children, abuse, race, gender, supervision and the media [Margaret Richards, 1989. Personal Communication NISW, 1989]. In recent years there has been a concentration on getting the procedures right as a means of handling this highly charged topic. Maureen Stone argues that these can never replace the need for developing a theoretical base which addresses a much wider context and complexity of factors than at present. Part of the analysis has to be a recognition that social workers and social care workers will not be able to eliminate child abuse and that while we must do our best to promote good practice and must be held to account for our work, responsibility for abusing children has to rest with the perpetrator.

The concentration on the family and family living as both the source of explanation and the only medium for intervention has impeded the development of methods and strategies. A recognition of the multi-causal nature of child abuse will release the constraints around the theories available for understanding and thus also the constraints on the range of options we need as practitioners and managers. An exclusive focus on the family not only contradicts the evidence but also can lead to stereotyping black and white women by placing responsibility on them for either (a) failing to stop physical abuse or (b) failing to know about sexual abuse. Similar stereotyping of black families can occur because of a failure to understand that physical and sexual abuse of children is unacceptable in all cultures.

Abuse also takes place outside the family; recent cases of child prostitution are but one example. Others include abuse by the very workers whose responsibility it is to protect children. This book recognises and discusses the fact that, like any other profession, membership and qualifications do not make us exempt from the pressures and feelings leading to abuse. Facing our own humanity and vulnerability is part of the task. This used to be known as self-awareness and however it is termed today using this as a major tool in the job of social work and social care remains relevant.

Good support systems are also essential and Maureen Stone gives 'tips' to workers on how to get the best out of available supervision.

She does not neglect the fact that managers need to take responsibility for ensuring that the usual supervisory structures are provided and, when necessary, there is access to a counsellor. There are certain occupational hazards such as threats of violence to workers and their children around which a wall of silence is often erected. Recognition that these exist and need to be catered for from time to time have to be part of the agenda. Otherwise workers carry as individuals, stresses which actually arise from the tasks they are required to carry out as part of the job. Some anticipatory work is better than trying to work through all this for the first time in the middle of a crisis.

Knowing the size and nature of the task in all its aspects is more likely to prepare us as individuals or teams of workers, supervisors or managers, than silence and avoidance. If we cannot name and face our own fears our service to children will inevitably be affected. The fear may be of violence towards ourselves or in some cases, as Maureen Stone points out, some white workers become paralysed because they fear being called racist. Black children then get a poorer and potentially a dangerous service.

Good child protection services will be good for all children. The Children Act 1989 creates a new balance between parents and their children, who are coming to be seen as citizens with rights. We are reminded in a historical discussion on protective measures, such as nineteenth century legislation, that removing young children from employment had the unforeseen consequence of reducing their rights. Maureen Stone gives us a valuable reminder that just as child abuse is multi-causal so, important though the new legislation is, it has to be accompanied by developments in theory, practice, supervision and management to ensure that these changes in the status of children have the intended impact on their day-to-day lives.

Daphne Statham, Director.
National Institute for Social Work.

Introduction

This book is divided into two parts, Part 1 offers a brief introduction to some of the historical and sociological factors which shaped the origins and development of Child Protection Work (CPW). It examines the theoretical and practical limitations of current thinking and suggests an analytical framework for understanding child abuse in contemporary society. After looking at the origins of CPW the focus shifts to an analysis of the work itself by means of job-analysis. This attempt to analyse child protection work in a systematic way should not be misinterpreted as reducing the work to a series of tasks and functions. On the contrary, the very complex and demanding nature of the work and the highly charged emotional atmosphere around it, suggest that such an approach is required.

Part 2 of the book is directly concerned with surviving in the field, focusing on the main factors affecting practice. The three chapters focus in turn on the contextual, professional and personal issues which impact on child protection work. Some themes occur in all three chapters for example, the social issues of gender, race and class. Some of the issues are sensitive and deal with matters which have been avoided in the past. However, the profession cannot afford to be squeamish about confronting its own shortcomings nor the human failings of some professionals. Social workers should have confidence in the child protection system in which they work, and confidence in the quality of service they are able to give.

Chapter 1

The Origins of Child Protection Work

'The gradual emergence of a more collectivist and interventionist state towards the end of the nineteenth century was accompanied by the increasing regulation by state of the family sphere. The moment when the state begins to have an open and direct stake in the family extends its powers of legal and administrative regulation, and begins to develop policies that have the family and family life as their object, is thus a critical one in the development of the modern state.' MacIntosh, *The Family, Regulation and the Public Sphere*.

' "I'm not sure whether I like that (the statutory) part of the work . . . . It is the community social work and the patch work which I enjoy, setting up projects, working alongside people. But then there is the other side, getting alongside people, getting to know a lot about them and then having to use that against them and take their children into care . . . um . . . I'm not happy about that." ' A social worker quoted in Stone, *Social Work Training for Child Protection Work*.

The above quotations encapsulate the two sides of the story – increasing state intervention in family life and the problems faced by those who actually have to implement state policies. The conflict which the social worker described above results from a number of factors, many of which will be addressed in the following pages. We start with a closer look at the nature and extent of the problems facing social workers in child protection work.

In a report into the death of Doreen Mason (who was killed by her parents whilst on an 'At Risk' Register), the Area Review Committee of the London Boroughs of Southwark, Lewisham and Lambeth (1989) criticised Southwark Social Services department for its 'siege mentality' and 'destructive mistrust' between senior managers. The report observed that Doreen's social worker was given no proper training or supervision; case conferences were not conducted or minuted properly, and time was wasted disputing which Local

Authority should manage the case. In October 1989 the Social Services Inspectorate (SSI) reported on its investigation into Cumbria Social Services handling of child abuse cases. The Inspectors found that there were potentially 'dangerous flaws' in the way some social workers responded to suspected cases of child abuse. There were 'potentially dangerous practices' in the identification of abuse, with 'shortcomings in both individual practices and management control'. Three years earlier, in 1986, the SSI reported on the social workers' handling of specific child abuse cases and expressed considerable concern over working practices and the management and supervision of practitioners.

It seems fair to say there are two sets of victims resulting from these terrible situations, abused children and the social workers who are meant to provide a child protection service. The quality of the service depends, to some extent, on the quality of the workers. This book is not simply about 'surviving child protection work', it is about offering a better child protection service as the basis of that survival. To achieve this end social workers must be prepared to ask questions – why were the Case Conferences not properly minuted? Why was the social worker not given proper training and supervision? Are trainers and the social work training establishments to blame for those 'potentially dangerous flaws and practices' which the SSI identified? This book sets out to encourage social workers to ask questions and make demands. This is the way to improve the quality of the service; to preserve the integrity of the professional and to reduce pressures on individual workers.

In this first chapter the origins of Child Protection Work in Britain are explored and its historical and sociological origins are identified and discussed. The limitations of social work theory in regard to Child Protection Work are also looked at and shown as being critical to a full understanding of the way that practice in this field has evolved. In Chapter 2 the nature of Child Protection Work itself is analysed and its component parts examined. There is a view that such analysis inevitably produces a mechanistic model which devalues the true nature of the 'people-centred' work, however there is also the possibility that this approach will bring to this field a structure and coherence which is too often missing. Child Protection Work has a very high emotional content which at times threatens to overwhelm practitioners. The hope is that if the nature of the job itself is better understood and the social work task more clearly defined, practitioners will be better placed to deal with the emotional aspects. Careful thought will show that there is a strong case for a structured, analytical approach to work which has a high emotional content.

There is nothing inherently limiting in this approach; an approach may be restrictive or helpful and this will depend entirely on how it is used. In the field of Child Protection Work a structured, analytical approach is necessary, not least as a support to those who daily confront the misery of victims; the demands of often unsupportive management and the attentions of a critical and sometimes hostile society. One thing should be clear from the start – this book does not offer practitioners a compilation of 'skills and techniques' which they can acquire in order to 'survive' child protection work. Although guidance, practical hints and other 'survival' strategies are included, these are not seen as very useful in themselves. The most important and critical thing is to get to grips with the underlying issues; social workers are then better placed to examine their own personal and professional approach, and to improve on their coping and survival skills.

A Definition of Child Protection Work
The legal definition of 'a child' is a person who has not reached the age of majority; in Britain the age of majority is eighteen years. The Shorter Oxford Dictionary defines 'to protect' as being 'to defend or guard from injury'; and among the meanings attributed to the word 'work' are 'to do, perform, practice' activities for which one receives payment. It therefore seems fair to define Child Protection Work as professional social work activities, the primary concern of which is to guard against, to prevent or to reduce the possibility of avoidable injury to children. The term 'injury' covers and includes not just physical injury but emotional and physical neglect, and all types of sexual abuse. These three activities constitute injury to a child. No attempt will be made to separate different types of abuse (eg sexual abuse) since such separation and splitting is considered unhelpful both to children and to professionals.

The definition of Child Protection Work offered is solely concerned with the professional activities of social workers and it is not a definition of 'child protection' *per se*. Child protection is an area of activity for many professionals, notably doctors, lawyers, police officers, teachers and other education personnel. Additionally, child protection should legitimately be the natural concern of all adult human beings, as part of their social responsibility towards the next generation. For present purposes, Child Protection Work is seen as part of professional social work practice and, as such, is quite distinct from any individual's own personal or private interest in children's well-being. Thr primary and over-riding concern of Child Protection Work is therefore to 'guard or defend children from injury'. The use of the term 'injury' may seem very limited in this context, but it has attractions: any form of abuse constitutes an injury to a person, be it mental, physical or psychological. To injure a person is to do them harm, any avoidable injury to children, therefore constitutes child abuse.

This book uses the term Child Protection Work, (usually abbreviated to CPW) rather than 'Child Abuse Work', because the concern here is with the protection of rather than the abuse of children. There is a problem over the use of the term 'child abuse' by social workers and other professionals. The following extract from a television discussion best serves to illustrate the problem. The discussion (BBC 2, 5 July 1989) followed the screening of a film about child sexual abuse within the family. Dr Wayatt, one of the paediatricians who were involved with the admission to hospital of a high number of Cleveland children because of suspected sexual abuse, (see the Report of the Inquiry in Child Abuse in Cleveland, HMSO, 1987) is a member of the discussion panel. Asked about his future, Dr Wayatt replied,

'I wish to continue to experience child sexual abuse (pause) as a health problem affecting children.'

And later on in the discussion, he stressed that,

'I have a continuing commitment to child abuse and think I have a contribution to make, albeit a non-clinical one at the moment.'

Anyone who followed the Cleveland affair cannot be in any doubt of what Dr Wayatt meant, and that his commitment is to child *protection* – however much his actual words belie this. These extracts show that professionals need to be careful in their use of certain terms and expressions, if they are to avoid confusing the issue even more. The use of the term 'Child Abuse' in the social work literature is also quite confusing and suffers from the problems highlighted in Dr Wayatt's interview. It is the intention in this book to use the term 'child abuse' to mean exactly what it says – the abuse of children. And the term 'child protection' to mean the protection of children from harm or injury. The use of such definitions helps to set limits, clarify meanings and to some extent, determine responses. If we used the term 'Child Abuse Work', what would this imply – that people are working at abusing children or to prevent the abuse of children? It is not clear. Are these social workers working with the abuser or the abused? The use of the term 'child abuse' in this context does not convey an implicit or explicit concern with the prevention of injury to children. The first survival skill which practitioners can usefully acquire is the precise and appropriate use of words in connection with their professional activities in this field.

To assist this process, trainers, writers of training material, researchers and other academics in this field are also encouraged to be more precise in their terminology. For example, books and articles with titles such as *The Management of Child Abuse*, BASW (1985); *The ABC of Child Abuse Work*, Moore, (1985); and *Child Abuse Risk and Resources*, Corby and Mills, (1986); should be discouraged – whereas 'Child Abuse – Working Together for the Protection of Children' would be a more appropriate title for any of the above. The misuse and over-use of the term 'child abuse' by professionals is worrying in that it gives a high profile to the negative aspect. The over-use of the term also feeds an unhealthy fascination with the subject. This point was made by a social services Training Officer who cynically observed that to ensure a good uptake on any training course, 'All you have to do is put "child abuse" somewhere in the title thus: Child Abuse (or even better Child Sexual Abuse) How to Complete Your Expenses Forms." Unfortunately, social workers in residential and fieldwork positions have abused children; and that is another good reason for being clear about how you use the terms 'child abuse' and 'child protection' in relation to social work.

The use of inappropriate and misleading terminology is not helpful in identifying the profession with clarity of aims and purpose. In an area highly charged with emotions, the use of terms which add to this highly charged atmosphere is to be discouraged. Child protection is also a more precise indication of the service being provided. To say that the social work profession is engaged in Child Abuse Work is to say that either it is reacting to the abuse of children, or actually causing child abuse! To say that the social work profession is engaged in CPW is to state that the social workers's job involves protecting children from avoidable and preventable injury, where these risks are known to exist. The 8th International Congress on Child Abuse and Neglect (planned to take place in 1990 after the completion of this book) will focus on 'Child Abuse or Child Protection – Society's Dilemma.' Professionals are adding to their own, and society's dilemma by this misuse of this term.

Child Protection Work – Historical and Sociological Background

> 'The movement for the protection of children has also been inspired by a growing sense of social solidarity which regards the welfare of the community as depending upon the welfare of the children so intimately that any injury inflicted upon children is transmitted to the whole community'. Rowan, 1982.

It is not possible to go into the details of how the present situation came about, but it is important to have some idea of the end result of the historical and sociological processes which resulted in present arrangements. Two major factors have influenced the development of Child Protection Work in Britain. First was the shift of power in the family, from men to women and, allied to the first change, was a further shift of power from women (i.e. mothers) to the State and its agents. Many who speculate about the uncovering of child abuse, especially within families, would perhaps understand these developments better if they placed them within their proper historical and sociological context. It is not that social workers and doctors have 'invented child abuse' in order to justify and legitimize their professional roles, although an element of 'professional expansionism' cannot be entirely discounted. Research by Dingwall *et al* (1983) has shown that the majority of children protection cases referred to Social Services Departments are pre-defined as such. Thus the initial task of the social worker is concerned with investigation rather than definition.

A more accurate view is that the extension of the Welfare State into family life has enabled aspects of family life to come under very close scrutiny. The development of the Welfare State brought women, as workers and as mothers, more and more into the public arena. Through education, health, social security and the welfare system, which all offered something to 'the family' and therefore brought women, as the main carers of the family, within their orbit, the family was accessed much more thoroughly than ever before. The Children Act (1989) is trying to redress the balance by shifting power back to parents, and conferring on the judicial system the role of arbitrator in disputes between the state (ie the Local Authority) and parents. The Association of Directors of Social Services (ADSS) in their Briefing Note No 9 on The Children Act (March, 1981) commented that the proposed changes will result in

> 'A noticeable shift towards parents and away from Local Authorities and towards the courts in decisions and in the resolution of disputed matters. The new law puts impressive responsibilities on parents to look after their own children but has expectations of parental behaviour which may not always be achieved by parents in acute personal need and deprivation.'

These comments illustrate the historical process which has been going on in relation to the State's involvement in child care and its intervention in family life. The first stage which occurred during the nineteenth century resulted in a shift of power away from the family and towards the State; and this most recent stage sees the attempt (by a government committed to reducing state power generally) to reverse or halt this process. Only time will tell what the results of this move will be and how it affects the lives of children. (See

MacCleod, (1982) for an analysis of the family in child care legislation and social work.)

The contemporary conflict over child protection – eg Cleveland – is part of a continuing conflict over child care. The history of child care policy and legislation affecting children has been characterised by conflict. Social work agencies, and social workers as child protection agents are inevitably caught up in these conflicts. This is the logical consequence of all that's gone before, which has contributed to the development of CPW as a part of professional social work practice.

The Origins of Child Protection Work

> 'Two events . . . have occurred in the past fifty years which have had a profound effect on child care legislation. Denis O'Neil, a foster child in the care of the local authority died in 1946 and Maria Caldwell died at the hands of her stepfather, while under local authority supervision.' Macleod, (1982).

Three factors were heavily implicated in the development of child protection work: firstly, the expansion of State intervention in family life; secondly, the extension of the period of 'childhood' and therefore of dependence; and thirdly, the increasing authority and influence of child care and medical professionals (together with improvements in X-ray and medical technology enabling better diagnosis of children's illnesses). These three factors are expanded below.

The Expansion of State Intervention in Family Life
The expansion of State power over the family was linked to the changing role of both the family and the State, and changes in the nature of society itself. Gradually the State accepted its child protection role and this was the major plank on which it extended its intervention into family life. (See Behlmer (1982) for an analysis of the development of child protection in Britain from 1870/1908.) By 1908 the State had taken to itself the power to remove children from their families. There were no major developments until after World War 2.

The murder of Denis O'Neill by his foster-father in 1946, resulted in renewed efforts to improve the lot of children, and 1948 saw the introduction of the first Child Care Statute, which brought into being the Local Authority Child Care Departments. The Maria Caldwell case was probably the next major landmark in the development of 'protective legislation'. Maria Caldwell was killed

7

by her stepfather whilst in the care of East Sussex County Council. (See *The Report of The Committee of Inquiry into the Care and Supervision provided in Relation to Maria Caldwell*, HMSO, 1974. See also *Child Abuse: A Study of Inquiry Reports*, HMSO, 1982; for a review of the findings of the child abuse inquiries.) The most recent major inquiry of this kind concerned Jasmine Beckford who was killed by her stepfather whilst she was in the care of the London Borough of Brent (*A Child In Trust*, London Borough of Brent, 1986). The Beckford case and the inquiry report has had a major influence on the child care policy and legislation.

Extension of the Period of 'Childhood' and of Dependence

It is a matter of historical record that once children were withdrawn from the labour force they ceased to exist as independent beings. As with so much in social policy, things did not develop as intended. The removal of children and young people from the work force for their protection may have also, inadvertently, diminished their rights and exposed them to other risks. The formal separation of childhood from work meant that children could no longer support themselves, or contribute towards the family upkeep; instead they were completely dependent on the family, the State or charity. This marked a significant change in the status of children, and we will return to this discussion later in relation to social workers' approach to child clients. It is important to note that these social and historical changes altered the relationship between the child and her/his family, especially among the working classes. Parents had different obligations and responsibilities towards children, whether they wanted them or not. Once these obligations were created, failure to fulfil them will result in State intervention and possible punitive action. For example, the law requires parents to send their children to school, failure to do this can have very serious consequences for parents and children.

This increased dependence of children on parents or other adults, is critically important because it points to a relationship between children and adults in which adults emerge, in all cases, as the most powerful group, with children always in a subordinate position. Adults and children stand in a power relationship to each other; in the case of adults this power is reinforced by their status as workers. With children, their lack of power is emphasised through their exclusion from the means of production – the world of work.

Growing Power and Influence of Professionals

The nineteenth and early twentieth century saw the development of new groups of professionals; among these were the social workers with a remit to improve the character of the poor. The voluntary sector in the form of The National Society For The Protection of

Children came into existence to fulfil this very role, but as the State increased its own powers the voluntary sector influence diminished.

At another level, child abuse was being formally discovered by the medical profession. In 1962, Dr Kempe and his colleagues published a paper in the *Journal of the American Medical Association*, in which they described the 'battered child syndrome'. The predisposing conditions linked to this syndrome were emotional but other deprivations were experienced by parents which resulted in their inability to provide proper care for their own children. Dr Kempe (1962) and his colleagues used psychotherapeutic treatment for parents so affected and estimated a success rate of 80%. The linking, by doctors, of child abuse to the early childhood experiences of the parents was very much in line with the thinking of social workers. Thus the medical and social work professions were, and are, united in their approach to child abuse as a family problem. There has been no major re-evaluation of this position by either group in the intervening years.

Changes in the Role and Function of the Family

In connection with the development of CPW it might be useful to consider some of the major changes which have affected the shape and size of the family in modern Britain. The 'family' was originally defined as any group of kin, but today is generally understood to mean a unit consisting of one or two adults and the resulting off-spring, including biological, adopted and step-children. The role, function and even the definition of 'the family' has undergone great changes in recent times.

In its present form, 'the family' in contemporary Britain is highly varied and diverse and generally less multi-functional than in the past, but smaller and more varied in its composition. In the past, the family was involved in a wide range of activities and family members had a variety of roles concerning these activities:

Economic – producing its own livelihood;
Social – producing entertainment;
Medical – health care of elderly, infants, children;
Welfare – providing care for the elderly, children, sick members.

In modern industrial societies the family is mainly a unit of consumption. Its main productive functions have become redundant as State, voluntary and private services have developed to replace them. Alongside these changes, society has also undergone another fundamental shift, from a religious to a secular society. This also encouraged the development of different types of behaviour and moral values in families and individuals. The emergence of an industrial society saw the development of social work and other professions, which also contributed to these social changes. New explanations of human behaviour were offered which appeared to suggest that people could control their own destiny, and need not be at the mercy of God or fate. The social work profession as it developed took over many of the welfare functions which the family had traditionally performed.

The following diagram will help to illustrate the developing and changing nature of the family, and will try to locate its historical role as a multi-functional productive unit, and its contemporary role as primarily a unit of consumption. In this process, the overall trend was for the family to become smaller, more isolated and more private. There are cultural and historical factors influencing the structure and composition of 'the family' in the racial, ethnic and religious groups which make up British society today. Even within the indigenous British population there are regional and class differences, but these observations are concerned with the generality and are intended to give a basic outline on how the role and function of the family has changed over time.

MacIver and Page's (1950) illustration shows how the productive functions of the family were gradually transferred to other agencies, the State, the voluntary and the private sectors. Family members looked to other sources for health-care, education, welfare provision, work, recreation and entertainment. The family's role became centralised on the production and rearing of children and the provision of psychological and emotional support to family members – based on the emotional and sexual relationship between two people – usually man and wife. The 1870 Education Act provided statutory education for working class children and thus effectively removed them from the care of their parents for a large part of the working day.

Some writers (e.g. Dale *et al*, 1981) have argued that a major role of family life is to provide emotional, psychological and sexual satisfaction to men and that State policies encourage the dependence of women on men. This could also explain the comments of a male judge when sentencing a man who had sexually abused his handicapped daughter. The judge took the view, that 'this healthy young man', having been denied sex with his wife because of her advanced state of pregnancy, *understandably* turned to his daughter for sex. ('Injudicious Record of Male Judges on Sexual Attacks' Sarah Boseley, *'The Guardian'*, 13 March 1989.) The judge seemed to be saying that sexual satisfaction is the right of all 'healthy young men' and the family is the obvious place to supply these needs. If the wife is ill she can pass the responsibility on to another family member. The family thus functions as a self-preservation unit, since the male head does not need to seek sexual satisfaction from outside it.

There is among some social workers a tendency to blame women for men's behaviour. Thus women who do not give their male

10

Emergence of the Modern Family Type – MacIver and Page

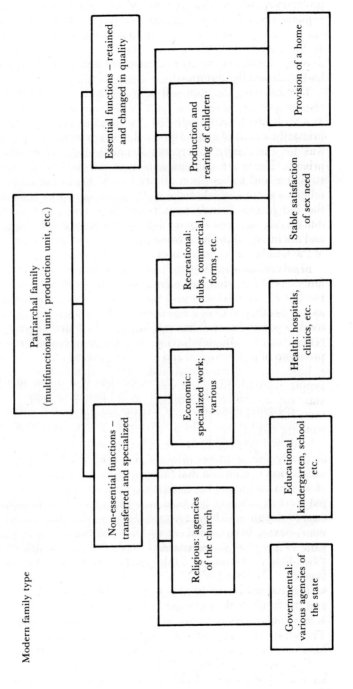

Modern family type

Patriarchal family
(multifunctional unit, production unit, etc.)

Essential functions – retained and changed in quality

Non-essential functions – transferred and specialized

Production and rearing of children

Provision of a home

Stable satisfaction of sex need

Religious: agencies of the church

Economic: specialized work; various

Recreational: clubs, commercial, forms, etc.

Governmental: various agencies of the state

Educational kindergarten, school etc.

Health: hospitals, clinics, etc.

partners sexual satisfaction are 'driving' them to incest and other types of sexual abuse. This blaming of women for men's behaviour has to be questioned, especially in relation to child sexual abuse. Fielding *et al* (1988) has defined child sexual abuse 'as overwhelmingly a male problem', and Newman (1989) provides confirmation of this. Newman also finds that abuse within the family constitutes only a percentage of this type of abuse. Newman's study related to young people who had run away from home or care. There were 93 cases (82 females) who reported that they had been sexually abused, (excluding prostitution). Rape and sexual abuse by non-family members accounted for 57; sexual abuse by a father 28, stepfather 3, other relative 13. Sexual abuse by both parents 1, and by mother 1. Sexual abuse within the family (i.e. by father or stepfather and the one mother) accounted for 25% of cases, with unknown male persons, other relatives and family friends accounting for 75%. There was no information linking the non-family abuse to any location – e.g. residential institutions.

In relation to abuse within the family, some social workers, believe that women often do know of sexual relations between their husbands, boyfriends or lovers and children (daughters/sons/stepchildren), but will tolerate, ignore or pretend to be ignorant of it. In social work jargon this has come to be known as 'the collusive mother/wife'. For women this means, as Fairtlough (1983) has pointed out, that both in social work theory and in practice they are the guilty ones:

> 'the real abuser in an incestuous family is the mother by frustrating her husband sexually, failing to support her daughter emotionally or foisting her duties and responsibilities on to her daughter, she engineers the incestuous relationship.'

The hard facts of many women's lives may be such that they cannot but 'collude' in some way in what is happening; at the same time as Fairtlough also has shown, there is abundant evidence to suggest that women in these circumstances do act to protect their children. But until the social and economic position of women considerably reduces their dependence on men, women have very little real choice one way or the other. This is manifested in their perception of their duty as being 'to keep the family together' at any cost.

The changing role of women has implications for the nature of family life and the care and protection of children. The General Household Survey (1989) preliminary analysis of life in Britain showed that 15% of families with dependent children were headed by single mothers. Even in two parent families men do not on a regular basis take responsibility for child care, and should the two parent family unit break down, it is the woman who is usually left

12

with sole responsibility for the children. The changing role of women and its effects on children presents female professionals with dilemmas. A female Equal Opportunities Officer refused to discuss with a female Social Services Manager the fact that an increase in child sexual abuse cases in the Borough was linked to women working in the evening leaving their male partners in charge of children, including putting them to bed. The EOPs Officer said that she 'did not want to know about that', her job is to increase women's choices, and she couldn't do this if she had to keep thinking about 'things like that'.

Child Protection Work resulted directly from changes in the role and function of the family and in the State's relationship to it. Under the patriarchal system, all formal power and control over the family – women and children – resided in male persons. Child protection as an area of professional activity did not exist, there were no child care professionals. As a result of industrialization and other forces, the nature of family life changed and men lost their right to the exclusive exercise of power and control over children. The role of women changed and women began to share some of that power and control over children. Women's access to power and control over children happened at a time when other changes resulted in increased professional interest in 'the family'. The involvement of mothers in the exercise of power and control over children facilitated an increase in State intervention in family life, as the professionals, teachers, social workers and doctors, targeted mothers as the means towards providing better health care, education etc for children.

Child Protection was, and remains, a central part of these developments – child protection was the means which the State used to intervene in family life. At the time of the patriarchal family there was minimal State intervention, but with the development of the smaller, more variable, and often female-headed family, State intervention increased. It has been suggested that the development of child protection as part of the increasing State intervention in family life was a direct result of the changing nature of the family and of the role of women, both in the family itself and in society generally. Although the origins of CPW may lie within the family, this is no reason why the parameters which define CPW in contemporary society should be limited to the family sphere. This approach has had important implications for social work practice in this field.

Social Work Theory and Child Protection Work

'In a social work context, this (i.e. the Freudian or casework) approach encourages a perception of the client as "victim" of his past, with three related elements: the identification of a problem through norm infraction; an

explanation presented in psychological or "scientific" terms; and a consequent attribution of non- or at least diminished responsibility to the client.'
Shepherd (1982)

Shepherd attacked social work theory for providing an explanation of human behaviour based on individual pathology, which at the same time denies that the individual is personally responsible for his/her own bad childhood experiences, which has left the abuser with many 'unmet needs' and the abuse is their way of meeting these 'unmet needs'.

In this sense, abusers (Shepherd calls all of them 'parents') are victims and the social work response is to care for them and help them to meet their needs in a less destructive way. Although control may also be used, such control is simply an aspect of the care being provided. This approach also embodies another fundamental principle of social work 'respect for persons'. Butrym (1976) defines respect for persons as 'a positive concern for them'. Many practitioners find these principles – if such they are – to be at odds with their feelings and reactions to the types of human behaviour encountered in CPW. They find no consolation or help from the body of professional literature which is intended to inform and guide their practice. And the victims of child abuse see such ideas as an added burden, increasing their sense of guilt. This is how a young mother who had been sexually abused by her own father for six years (from the age of six) commented on the social work view as she understood it:

'They say its because of his childhood, but its not true he had a happy childhood, my nan and grandad are lovely people . . . . they did not abuse him. Its all been gone into by social services . . . . he was not abused or ill-treated. But he abused me for six years . . . . and now they say that if you've been abused you will abuse your child. How can they say that? My dad was not abused, yet he abused me . . . . its not fair. How can they say that?'

Mass's (1989) critique of existing social work theory on parenting in relation to child abuse supports this survivor's views. Mass has called for a 'new paradigm shift' in social work theory arguing that current theoretical models fail to explain child abuse and in particular that:

'The adherence to the law of maternal instinct has . . . . attempted to explain child abuse as pathology by searching for the personal attributes of abusive parents . . . . and has placed child abuse under the influence of the medical ideology.'

Mass argued that personal pathology, as an explanation for child abuse, is an unsupported theory which gives comfort to those who explain human behaviour in terms of biology and undermines the humanistic basis of the social work profession. She questions the view that abusive behaviour is linked to experience of abuse and dismisses what she calls 'the unfounded thesis of the inter-generational cycle of abuse'.

MacLeod and Saraga (1988) reviewed the literature on child sexual abuse and identified three major theoretical perspectives: the libertarian, the psychoanalytical, and the family dysfunctional. They also noted the emergence of a feminist approach. But they concluded that in Britain the 'family dysfunction approach currently holds the position of orthodoxy among professionals'. What these writers call the 'family dysfunction' approach in fact may include psychoanalytical theory. In practice there are no neat dividing lines between approaches, and social workers base their practice on a mixture of ideas culled from different theories. The point is that even in the area in which social work claims most expertise, 'the family', the explanations of child abuse are inadequate to say the least.

In the wider social context, social work theory is deficient in the way it conceptualizes child protection issues. This means that social work practice in this field has an inadequate and impoverished theoretical base. The reasons for this are rooted in the historical and social context within which both the social work profession and the abuse of children have developed. The practical side of social work had its origins in charitable and philanthropic activities concerned with relieving poverty and poor housing in Victorian Britain. But the social work profession looked to Freudian psychology for its theoretical underpinning. So there was an inherent tension between the theory and practice of social work right from the very start. See Woodroofe (1974) for an historical account of the development of social work in Britain and the USA.

In recent times social work has sought to adapt its theoretical base by developing practice based on notions of 'community' and 'parti-cipation'. This approach was largely a reaction to 'centralised hierarchic organisations', (Hadley and McGarth, 1981). The alter-native approach, as outlined by Hadley and McGarth advocates the 'decentralisation of services to small units and the fusion of statutory work with voluntary action in the community'. These ideas were later to form the basis of what is now called community social work. The social worker quoted at the start of this chapter was discussing the conflict between the values and methods of community social work, and those of CPW. The problems and difficulties of applying a 'Community Social Work' model in the context of CPW will be discussed more fully in Chapter 5. For the moment Community Social Work is located within a methodology which stress 'collective' as opposed to 'individual' responsibility; and where the focus of intervention is more likely to be groups and neighbourhoods than individuals and families. Community Social Work relies on the notion of 'participation' with professionals and local communities working together to solve social problems.

The historical origins of social work theory and contemporary attempts to adapt, have only caused problems for practitioners and have often added to existing confusion, particularly in relation to child protection. These issues can best be illustrated with reference to, firstly, origins of social work theory in Freudian psychology and, secondly, in relation to the development of 'community social work'. At the NSPCC (1988) Conference-Treatment Approaches To Child Sexual Abuse, the keynote speaker, Professor Olive Stevenson, suggested that many of the problems which social workers experience in carrying out their child protection duties are due in a large part to the unresolved nature of many of their own childhood problems. No research or other evidence was given, and no supporting documentation was quoted from any of the numerous reports and inquiries which have been undertaken in this field. These views reflect the continuing influence of Freudian theory on contemporary social work.

Recent attempts to develop a more relevant theoretical approach to contemporary social work practice has had equally problematic results for practitioners. 'Community Social Work', based on notions of participation and community involvement poses particular problems in relation to CPW. The debate over how social workers can at one and the same time practice Community Social Work and carry out their child protection duties, split the Barclay Committee, (1984). People may be drawn to social work seduced by the 'participatory' community models, only to find themselves carrying out investigative and policing functions. For some this creates tensions, leads to low morale, and contributes to wastage through such people leaving the profession. Community social work does offer a positive approach to working with people, and may contribute towards the reduction of child abuse which is stress-related (i.e. physical abuse/neglect). Its role is less clear when preventative measures fail – how and when does the friendly neighbourhood social worker become a child protection officer? Do all social workers manage the role change with equal calm and competence?

In the area of child sexual abuse, the community social work approach becomes very problematic – how does a social worker carry out community social work on an estate where child sex rings are going on? Especially when the 'estate' is not in the working class, inner city areas but in prosperous middle class Surrey? In the summer of 1989, the Metropolitan Police were actively involved in investigating child sex rings in Weybridge, Feltham and Richmond – all mainly middle class areas. Social workers feel exposed and inadequate when confronted by the scale and prevalence of all types of child abuse; they are particularly ill-prepared for working with middle class communities. Community social work methods assume that the work is being carried out in working class, poor and deprived areas.

In addition, social work theory is deficient in providing practitioners with the knowledge, skills and understanding which will enable them to be effective child protection practitioners. Partial, selective and inadequate explanations are offered for complex and complicated issues; it is no wonder that practitioners feel lost and cling to any new fad or idea which seems to present an answer. What is required is a coherent theory which explains abuse and injury to children based on all the relevant factors – historical, social, cultural and economic. This should result in a more balanced view of the causes of child abuse and a more informed professional and productive response.

There has always been enormous tensions between social work theory and practice, springing from the historical origins of the profession: viz. servicing the poor but built on theories which came from men of rich and powerful backgrounds. The theories which formed the basis of the social work profession took little account of social issues. Problems of abuse, injury and neglect of children are explained primarily as a consequence or parental inadequacies and individual pathology. Gibson (1989) commenting on the origins of social work, stated that:

> 'Historically social work emerged in the *nineteenth century as a rescue service for the poor* (author's emphasis) . . . . .
> Ironically the focus was on the individual woman and *her* inadequacies and not on the economic social and cultural factors which might explain her inadequacies . . . . . a pattern of expectations about the female client was set up which is still evident in social work today.'

The origin of social work theory in Freudian psychology has had important implications for the profession. This influence has not diminished, and its effects in the field of child protection work remains considerable. To illustrate with an anecdote, during a visit to one of the largest and most prestigious children's hospitals in the United States, the author discussed with the Director of the Hospital Social Work Department the kind of child protection cases being dealt with by her department. She said that the sexual abuse of children was the most frequent, distressing and demanding task confronting the social workers in her department. When asked about training, the response came – currently the department had a good training programme, but unfortunately she herself had missed out on it, being as she said 'higher management'. What about the training she had herself received, had it prepared her for that kind of work?

'No, we were taught about the Oedipus complex – we knew that girls fantasise about sexual intercourse with their fathers – but there was nothing about genital herpes – I had no idea . . . .'

And now consider this statement made by two senior social workers who were involved in working with the victims of a ritualized (satanic) child abuse ring:

> 'It was difficult to hear properly at first – difficult to grasp how evil people can be. The social work profession derives from an optimism and belief in the innate potential for good and for change. Some of the disclosures made us physically ill . . . . grieving for the irretrievable loss of innocence and trust.'
> Dawson and Johnson 'When The Truth Hurts',
> (*Community Care* 30 March, 1989)

If all your training prepared you for was the fact that girls fantasise about sex with their fathers; and when proper training becomes available you are too high in management to qualify – heavens help you! Part 2 deals with training and related matters in more detail. But to return to definitions of child abuse. The Children's Legal Centre (CLC) in a pamphlet with the unfortunate title *Child Abuse Procedures* (1988) states that:

> 'Child abuse – sexual, physical and emotional – is often the most appalling symptom of the misuse of adult power over children – the result of adults' failure to respect the rights, autonomy, physical integrity and privacy of the child. It is usually perpetrated by people who are in a position of authority over the children they abuse. There is a common chord in the attitudes to children which lead to sexual, physical and emotional abuse, and the attitudes which lead to action believed to be in the child's 'best interests' which actually further abuses them: it is an assumption of authority which does not respect the child as a person with rights and views.'

The views expressed in the CLC's pamphlet are supported by the findings of inquiry reports into the death, injury and sexual abuse of children; newspaper reports on court appearances of people charged or convicted with these offenses and confidential information from various sources including social services departments. Systematic analysis of the relevant literature leads to a multi-causal explanation of child abuse, only some of which are associated with 'the family'. This means the social work view of child abuse, as 'a family problem', is inherently flawed and gives practitioners a very inadequate basis for their CPW. Any theory which tries to explain child abuse must deal with all its manifestations, accepting the complex and diverse nature of this phenomena. Social work must move towards an approach to CPW based on a more complete understanding of the critical factors involved in all types of child abuse.

The framework below is offered as a possible first step.

A Framework for the Analysis of Child Abuse

Type of abuse	Causal factors	Location	Perpetrated by
emotional abuse neglect	adult emotional and psychological problems	depends on access to children	parents/relative friends, other carers eg childminders
physical abuse and neglect	as above + social economic, political and environmental problems	families, schools, institutions	as above + teachers, Residential Staff etc
sexual abuse and exploitation	as above + personal preferences of adults (mostly males)	depends on access to children	all the above + those with a commercial interest

The advent of the video and VCR and the development of the child pornography market, has dramatically changed the nature of child sexual abuse, not just in Britain, but world wide. Just as victims may be any child, so perpetrators may be any adult.

Social workers must move away from the exclusive focus on the family and develop an analysis of child abuse which reflects the reality of life in contemporary Britain. Please note that strictly speaking, child abuse must include all avoidable harm caused to children by, for example, living in damp and dangerous conditions and exposure to toxins and other pollutants. These problems are not the specific remit of the social work profession, they should be of concern to society as a whole.

There is abundant evidence to show that child abuse is not exclusively or mainly a family problem. In Canada, The Badgley Commission Report (1984) documented many examples of the sexual abuse and exploitation of Canadian children in many areas of their lives. In Britain, there have been recent moves to protect children from sexual and other types of abuse in private schools and residential establishments. *Community Care*, (18 May, 1989) carried a report under the headline 'Move to Protect Children in Private

19

Residential Schools' and outlines moves by Ms Shepperd MP, to protect children in these schools, because she was:

> 'concerned to stop the kind of case which occurred recently at a special private school at Ludlow. Its co-proprietor had been charged with 14 offenses of sexual abuse involving pupils.'

At around this same time, the founder of Childline (The BBC Children's Telephone Helpline), Esther Rantzen was calling for the Children Bill to give power to Local Authorities to inspect private schools, (BBC1, *That's Life*, 11 June, 1989) following allegations of sexual abuse of pupils by the headmaster and staff of one such school. *The Independent* (9 December, 1989) recently reported that police, social services and Childline were agreed that child sexual abuse occurs in 'possibly 75% of boarding schools'. Although there are 'no solid statistics', the experiences of these agencies suggest that the figures are in that order of magnitude, and they called for a national intelligence unit to be set up to combat paedophilia. Mr Peter Bibby, Deputy Director of Social Services in the London Borough of Brent agreed with the estimate, and said that:

> 'The evidence is anecdotal, but I am speaking from a background of 25 years in social work, working for Dr Barnado's, in prisons and for Brent.'

The report quoted Mr Gasper, a detective chief inspector with the Metropolitan Police, who cracked a fifteen strong London sex ring in 1987, as saying that

> 'Paedophiles will manoeuvre themselves into situations where they come into contact with potential victims. That makes all caring organisations at risk of paedophiles. Maybe we will even see the police inadvertently recruiting them now that they are dealing so much with child sexual abuse.'

The report continued with another quote from Ms Howrath, Director of Childline, in which she said 'That statistic of 75% would not surprise me. The incidence in these schools is very high.' She said that teachers and children who know about the abuse do not report it because of feelings of guilt. She also said that some parents did not show any concern and reacted to sexual abuse in boarding schools as 'par for the course.' But it is not just boarding schools, there are well documented cases of physical and sexual abuse of children in local authority care. It is ironic that at the same time as the government is being asked to extend the local authority's power to inspect private schools and residential establishments, that there are similar calls for inspection of Children's Homes in Lambeth and Birmingham.

A recent survey of the young homeless in London found that 40% had run from local authority care. This is a serious indictment of the residential child care sector since only 1% of children are in care. The Kincora Boy's Home Scandal provides further evidence, if evidence is needed, of the dangers to children in local authority care. The allegations are that Kincora boys were used to entrap homosexual men for purposes of blackmail. Three senior members of staff of Kincora have been jailed, including the warden and his deputy; and three ex-inmates have received out of court compensation payments. Four separate inquiries have failed to reveal the truth about Kincora, and another one is requested. See the 'Kincora scandal lingers on.' *The Guardian*, 23 October, 1989.

A more recent example of institutional child abuse concerns Birmingham Social Services. Ms Adrainne Jones, Birmingham's Director of Social Services, expressed her sense of anger that 'children in Birmingham's care were the subject of abuse by our own staff.' (*Birmingham Daily News*, 12 September, 1989 'Council chief tells of anger on abuse.') At least Birmingham has been willing to admit that this has occurred and has since appointed a solicitor to investigate all allegations of physical and sexual abuse by staff of children in their care. In some local authorities allegations of abuse against staff are dealt with under industrial relations procedures and are, therefore, not classified as child abuse. The author has been reliably informed that some local authorities also reserve the classification 'child sexual abuse' for abuse within the family. All other types of sexual abuse are classified as 'sexual assault'.

In personal communications with the author a number of experienced child protection workers have said that they have never been involved with a non-family child sexual abuse case – even though they knew that such incidents had occurred. They just did not know what happened in these cases. Another example of this screening out process was provided by a senior practitioner who told of an incident where a five year old client of hers, living in a Children's Home, was made to stand partly naked in a cold and windy corridor as 'punishment' for being cheeky. The child became seriously ill with pneumonia and the social worker made a formal complaint. She received no reply for a long time and when she eventually enquired about what was happening, she was told that it was not right for fieldworkers to interfere with the management of residential institutions. As the child protection worker she felt that the child's punishment amounted to abuse. A view which must have been shared by the residential social work colleague who had told her about the abuse in the first place.

Social Services Departments must accept the implications and the consequences of these practices. Such practices are very harmful to the development of a comprehensive child protection service. A recent Social Services Inspector's report (1989) points out that social workers must consider all sources of possible abuse. This means that they must consider 'access' as a critical factor. Take 'C', a six year old girl, removed from home due to sexual abuse. She was placed in a foster home and the family were allowed supervised access. The father denied the abuse but the social worker was convinced of his guilt, so the father's visits were always closely supervised. Grandfather was left alone with the little girl during his access visits. After one such visit the foster-mother reported that the child's knickers were soiled and bloodied. It turned out that the grandfather had been sexually abusing the child all along. It seems obvious that the question 'who has access to the child'? should be amongst the first questions to be asked. If the child is in Day/ Residential Care, in a Play Group or with a Child Minder, all these people must be investigated and ruled out.

The fact that abuse occurs in all contexts must be actively borne in mind when taking abused children into care and in making placement decisions. Placements must be closely monitored and supervised, with social worker visits not always pre-arranged. This has implications for the relationship with foster-parents, but it is necessary. An SSD recently found out that a 'specialist' child sexual abuse foster family was nothing of the kind. The foster-father had been sexually abusing the children over a period of years; these facts came to light purely by accident and the man is now facing charges. In November 1989 a foster-mother was sentenced to life imprisonment for murdering a foster-child; eight years previously she had attacked another child but this had gone unnoticed (Inquiry follows foster killing, *The Guardian* 5 December, 1989). No child protection service can avoid such tragedies but progress towards a better system is hindered by a reluctance to face the true nature and complexity of the problem.

Summary of the Main Points
This chapter gave a brief outline of the background to the development of CPW in Britain. Changes in the role and function of the family and in relations between the family and the State were examined and their implications discussed. CPW resulted from these changes and, consequently, social work explanations of child abuse have focused on 'the family'. The result has been a partial and incomplete account which has impoverished the very basis of the child protection service.

A more complete theory of child abuse is urgently required, this must relate its occurrence to economic, political, social and other factors, as well as to 'family dysfunction'. Abuse may occur in the family, in the community, in day and residential institutions and even in church and other settings. Abuse may be perpetrated by any adult with access to children. The power of adults and the powerlessness of children would seem to be the most critical causal factor in all forms of child abuse. Although child abuse is an age old problem, there are aspects of contemporary life which appear to carry particular risks to children: e.g. high levels of alcohol and drug abuse; serial marriage; 'reconstituted family' (i.e. one resulting from the divorce and remarriage of the partners). Affluence and poverty may carry equal but different risks.

A very rudimentary framework for the analysis of child abuse was presented in this chapter. Such analytical tools may be helpful to practitioners who are in danger of being overwhelmed as they struggle to improvise adequate responses to complex problems. Practitioners are often impatient with 'theory' and anxious to get on with 'doing' things: 'helping' people; 'protecting' children. But actions not informed by careful thought and the use of available knowledge, not only fail to benefit the client, but also leave the social worker exposed and very vulnerable.

The main topics examined and discussed in this chapter were:

1) The misuse of the term 'child abuse' was discussed, and it was suggested that the term child abuse should not be used inappropriately, as for examine in 'child abuse procedures'.

2) Child Protection Work (CPW) as it is currently undertaken in Social Services Departments and the NSPCC is the result of historical processes, of which the development of professional social work is but one.

3) Social work theory is deficient and inadequate in its explanation of the origins and causes of child abuse. This theory deficit has had major implications for social workers, leaving them to cope as best they can, and to blame themselves (unresolved childhood problems?) when they fail to perform adequately.

4) Changes in the family role and function of the family, and of women are also relevant to this discussion. It was suggested that social changes affecting the family in general, and women in particular, were the main determinants leading to the development of child protection as a function of the State; and to CPW as a major part of professional social work.

5) Children can be abused by any adult who has power and control over them, be they parents or professionals. The abuse of

institutional and professional power may also contribute to the suffering and distress of children. This is shown by the increasing evidence of child abuse – including sexual abuse in State and private institutions.

6) Child abuse is associated with a number of social, economic, environmental, political, personal and family factors, but overriding all these is the total dependence of children on adults and the amount of power adults have over children – whether as parents, or as parent-substitutes, or simply as people whose greater physical strength and knowledge and experience gives them power in situations involving children. No distinction was made between different types of child abuse – the deciding criterion in defining child abuse being anything which causes injury and avoidable harm to children.

Chapter 2
The Nature of Child Protection Work
Defining the Client and the Task

Gelles and Cornell (1985) described two approaches to detecting, investigating and responding to child abuse, one they termed a 'humanistic model', and the other a 'control' model. The humanistic approach which is seen as characteristic of social workers and other human service professions, has 'a non-punitive outlook with an abundance of human kindness . . . . . . compassionate intervention involves supporting the abuser and his or her family. Home-maker services, health and child care, and other supports are made available to the family.' In contrast the 'control model' involves 'aggressive use of intervention to the limit and, if necessary, punishing the deviant violent behaviour.' In casework theory, 'control' is treated simply as an aspect of 'care'.

In keeping with the received orthodoxy Gelles and Cornell approached child abuse purely as a family problem, and diagnosed the professional responses in those terms. In recent years there have been major scandals in the USA involving the sexual abuse of children in day nurseries. Anyone carrying out research in this field cannot be unaware of the fact that there is growing evidence of abuse of all types happening in these institutions. Bowlby's (1953) research, on which he based his theory of 'maternal deprivation', was more about the poor standards of child care in institutions than about maternal deprivation. The literature of nineteenth century Britain is full of stories, poems and other records of the violence and oppression suffered by children, in workhouses, on farms and in factories. Against this background how and why did the abuse of children come to be defined mainly as a 'family problem' and why has child protection come to be viewed in such narrow terms? Are these limitations in the way child abuse is perceived linked in any way to problems in the practice of child protection work?

In trying to reach some understanding of the social work task in child protection work, it is necessary to move away from current thinking; the view which will be taken here is that children are at risk of abuse and injury both from within and outside the family.

Therefore child protection work must be concerned with the nature and scope of abuse of children and young persons in all social contexts. This may make it possible both to lessen the chances of further abuse and to improve the chances of improved job satisfaction for social workers. Social workers often seem to place job satisfaction very low on their list of priorities, especially in the area of child protection work. It should be very high; strategies to promote job satisfaction are also very likely to be associated with good outcomes for the client and the agency.

The so-called 'humanistic approach' to child protection work which is described above is a confused and muddled response; which exposes the social worker to demands she cannot hope to fulfil. The social worker defines the cause of the abuse, and then works, not to protect the child but to assist the 'sad, needy, deprived human beings' who have been defined as the perpetrators. Child protection work is what it says, it is about protecting children, and the same worker who is meant to be protecting the victim cannot also succour the attacker. Such roles are incompatible and should not be expected of any professional. It is simplistic and divisive to define different types of professional responses as 'humanistic' and 'controlling', as though these were mutually incompatible concepts. Anyone accused or suspected of abusing or injuring children has legal rights and is not, by virtue of such accusations or suspicions, 'a client' of social services departments. Once child protection work is properly defined and its remit clearly understood, the social workers professional relationship with others should become less confused.

Two illustrations show how loosely the term 'client' is used in social work. Corby's (1988) research report, a study of how social workers dealt with child abuse cases, provides the first illustration. At one point the author, a social work lecturer, discusses the position of parents under investigation for alleged abuse of their children. Having observed the difficult position of parents accused or suspected of abusing their children, the author says, 'Clearly this is a problem for all agencies and training could overcome some of these difficulties.' Corby suggests that the way an agency handles these 'clients' is 'likely to colour the client's impression of other agencies as well as have negative consequences for future work.' Parents have been given the status of 'clients' whether or not they are in fact clients in the accepted sense of the word. The second example is drawn from a report on 'Practice and Procedures', Westminster City Council (1986). The authors discuss practice issues and focus on developing an open partnership with 'the client':

> 'Practice is about 'how' things are done rather than 'who does what and when' which is procedure. Clarity, purpose, careful planning, skilled assessment, constant re-evaluation and an open partnership with the clients.'

Although the whole statement is not very clear in itself, it is clear on the identity of the 'clients', without doubt these are the parents of child abuse victims. Later on the authors of the Westminster Report draw attention to the role of the social worker in monitoring the health of the parents of children at risk of abuse. The report states (page 35)

> 'The health of the parent is frequently an important issue in families with children being, or at risk of being, abused. The EPT (Evaluation Project Team) considers that a record of the parents' health is important information and must not be ignored.'

These same parents are 'open partners', involved in decision-making, attending, at least in part, case conferences and reviews and, there again, their health records are being monitored to provide an indication of when they are next likely to abuse their children. This creates a situation of role confusion and conflict for both the parent and the professionals. Social workers are asked to take contradictory roles when dealing with parents; and there appears to be no distinction made between the parent who may be an interested party (in being a suspect) and those who are not. These confused and conflicting demands made of social workers, particularly when they may also be in potentially dangerous and violent situations, add to role conflict and demoralisation. Thus the Westminster report continues:

> 'Abusing families are often violent families. Social workers who come into the lives of these families are often subjected to physical threat. There is no clear departmental policy that guides or protects social workers in these situations . . . . . . In our survey 40% of respondents reported that they had been physically threatened in relation to their child abuse case load. A large number described these incidents in detail, and some included threats of murder.'

It can be seen that the issues we are discussing here may be really quite central to the social workers' physical survival as well as their survival as competent professionals. It is also clear that the Westminster Working Party which compiled this document saw neither the inherent contradictions in what they were saying nor the fact that they were often in danger of adding to existing problems by confused and muddled thinking. Having identified 'clarity of purpose' as one of the major components of good practice in this field, the writers go on to confuse the reason for the intervention with other related but secondary issues, thereby losing sight of child protection as the central issue. Louis Blom-Cooper chaired two inquiries into the abuse of children in Local Authority care. In a report in *The Guardian* 8 June, 1986 he is quoted as saying

'. . . . . . sympathy for the abusing parent can, and frequently does lead social workers to focus on them rather than on the child. The only safe path for the profession of social work to follow is for its practitioners to look first and foremost to the law . . .'

BASW (1985) endorses this, its code of practice encourages child protection agencies and their workers to regard the child, not the parents, as the 'primary client'.

These are complex and difficult problems. It is not being suggested that child protection can be carried out without reference to the social situation (including the family life of the children concerned), what is being suggested is that, where abuse is taking place within the family, the focus of child protection work is the protection of the child/children. Practitioners must tidy up their use of language, particularly the way they define people as 'clients'. Gillner and Morris (1981) showed how local authority social workers supervising delinquent adolescents included the whole family, and especially the mother, within the supervision process – often at the expense of contact with the designated client. In comparison Probation Officers focus directly on the offender as 'the client' and their interventions are generally more productive as a result.

The question is – what professional approach is to be adopted by social workers? Labelling 'suspects' as 'clients' puts them into a dependent relationship with the social worker, assumes that they want to be 'a client', that they understand what that means, and that they accept the changes implied in relation to the social worker. It is fundamental to the approach adopted in this book that in child protection work, the child is the client of the child protection agency. Other individuals involved may become clients of other social workers or agencies, but the child protection worker should not define or categorise others as their 'clients' in the process of carrying out their child protection work. This point is also relevant in relation to parents' rights to attend or be represented at Case Conferences. Clearly where the parent/s or guardian/s are not suspected of being involved in the abuse, their role is entirely different, they are not a party to the proceedings other than as the parent/s and the person/s primarily responsible for the child's well-being. One could argue that in normal circumstances it is difficult to see any good reason for excluding parent/s from case conferences. The Children Act (1989) will alter the relationship between the local authority and parents and should promote clarity and reduce the amount of confusion in this area.

Where the parent/s are party to the action, either by virtue of being under suspicion or by an admission of guilt, the situation changes. The parent/s are interested parties in their own right – their freedom and liberty may be at stake. It is difficult to see how under these circumstances, and given the formal remit of case conferences, it can be helpful for parents to be present and to take part. Yet this does happen, and this process has developed without proper discussion, evaluation or reflection as to its purpose and consequences. It may be that such a reflective process would result in the same outcome, but at least there would be the confidence that the right questions had been asked and considered from the start. Like so much in social work there is a tendency to act from good intentions, without subjecting ideas to critical scrutiny and with the acceptance of the fact that the best intentions may have negative as well as positive outcomes. It is not enough to be well intentioned, proposals must be examined and analysed in a process which includes consultation with those likely to be affected, testing these against the agency's aims and goals.

There is an urgent need for clarity in these and related matters. Insistence on the correct terminology is very important in helping to promote clarity and lessen confusion. The difficulties which social workers encounter in defining the child as 'the client' are not underestimated, and this will be discussed in the next section. It is acknowledged that in order to treat the child as the client, the social worker may have to put her/his feelings and views on 'hold', in the interest of focusing on the child protection issues. The inquiry into the death of Jasmine Beckford left many social workers feeling betrayed by their beliefs and the efforts they make to protect children. The focus on supporting these 'deprived, inadequate, needy' parents is not the same as protecting the vulnerable child. Since the world is far from perfect and social workers are limited in what they achieve, they have no choice but to put their maximum effort into protecting children.

It is necessary to distinguish between the interests of adults, including social workers, and the interests of children. Some practitioners may be worried that this implies not working with parents – even non-abusing parents – but it does not. What it should ideally do is to clarify the reasons for such involvement and the terms on which parent/s become a party to action to rescue or rehabilitate their children. A senior social worker illustrates how this can be achieved. In discussing a case in which the mother consistently focused on her own problems, pushing the child protection issue, the reason for social work involvement, aside – this is how the social worker outlined her approach:

> 'I explained to her that the purpose of our meetings was to help Mary recover from her awful experiences, and that I needed her help if this was to be done. I accepted that she also needed help, but said that I felt that it

would not be right for me to be the one to attempt both things . . . . . . she seemed to understand and accept this.'

Some practitioners may disagree with this and feel that the child's interests would be best served through helping the mother. However, experience has shown that these boundaries are necessary if the child is to be the focus of child protection work.

Children and Social Work – the Child as Client

Whatever legislative or procedural changes may be introduced to ensure that children are consulted and that their wishes are taken into account in decisions which affect them, the fact remains that legal and procedural guidelines are implemented by professionals whose values and attitudes affect the implementation process. In the nature of things, it is understandable that social workers often experience very real problems seeing and treating children as clients. These problems spring from many sources – some of the historical details have already been discussed. The implications of this history of social work has been that 'the family' is what social workers know and feel competent to deal with. Hence, as suggested earlier, there is a tendency to define problems, whatever their origins, in terms of 'the family'. (See *Gillner and Morris*, 1982, for a fuller discussion of these matters.)

In CPW the problem is compounded by another factor – the social and legal status of children and young people and the way various agencies treat young clients. Problems can occur between child protection workers and workers in other agencies over this very matter. For example, another worker in an Intermediate Treatment (IT) or Youth Work setting makes a referral to Social Services based on a prior agreement with the child/young person concerned. Once the referral has been made the IT worker finds that the undertaking given to the young person has no validity and that the Social Services will take what action they think fit. This leaves the IT worker exposed and angry and reduces the possibility that s/he will approach social services again. Yet it seems quite clear that if the child/young person is the true client, then their views and wishes should be paramount, and everything possible should be done to respect them. This problem has also affected the relationship between Social Services Departments and new specialist services for abused children. When Childline was first established there was a reluctance to refer children to some SSDs because there were no guarantees that promises made to the children would be respected. It is not clear how far the problems have been resolved.

The status of children and young persons in contemporary British society is problematic. On the one hand, children and young people

30

are targeted as consumers. They are under constant pressure from advertisers and retailers to buy things and this gives them the same 'consumer' status as adults – at least, the ones who have money to spend. On the other hand their dependency is extended by laws which prolong the period of childhood, including compulsory education to age sixteen (eighteen if a university education is desired) and social security changes. Historically, 'childhood' has undergone many changes; as society becomes more complex, the expectations of and the pressures on children change. Social work professionals are affected by these changes and their views and expectations of children and young people reflect these social influences.

In general these factors – the professional interest and inclination of social workers to work with families and the marginalisation of children – make it very difficult for social workers to treat children and young people seriously as clients. By the age of eight children are probably much like other people in the way they behave. They tell lies, change their minds, have conflicting loyalties, don't want to upset things – or conversely want to upset things – just like adults. There is no reason to treat children differently from other people, they are not less than other people because they are smaller. What has to be taken into account is the circumstances in which anybody, adult, child or young person is placed, the pressures on them, how able or not they are to withstand these pressures and what help and support they may need to cope with their situation.

It may be helpful to look at what other professionals have found in their attempts to work directly with children as clients. L. Perry, Official Guardian for children for the State of Ontario in Canada, wrote a paper *Independent Representation for Children in Neglect and Abuse Cases* (1983). Writing about the development of a child's counsel Perry reflected on the historical background, in these words:

> 'Traditionally child welfare agencies were the accepted representatives of the child's best interest. They spoke for the child before the court. The child's views, attachments and attitudes were considered by the agency, and might, or might not be included in the final recommendation to the judge . . . . . . Without the child being represented there is no guarantee that the investigation conducted by the agency and the resulting recommendation will be objective, complete or necessarily represent the best plan for the child.'

Perry glosses over the problems which have resulted in the establishment of an independent counsel for children in Ontario. By implication it seems that he is saying that welfare agencies could not be relied upon to represent the child's best interest, although they had the power to speak for children and to make recommendations to judges. However, as he says, without independent representation they could not be sure that the child's 'views, attachments and attitudes' would be considered. Hence the child became a direct client of the legal services and the lawyer took on the job of representing the child. Although child/young persons in Ontario had long had the right to legal representation in juvenile delinquency cases, there was no statutory provision for such representation in 'welfare matters' prior to 1978. In coming to a decision about whether to appoint an independent counsel for the child, the court has to decide whether in its opinion, there is a difference between the views of the child and society, and/or the child and the parents.

Perry comments that 'a major question in the minds of both child welfare workers and the legal profession is how does the lawyer represent the child? What does he represent? . . . . . . To assist the court and to adequately represent the child, does the lawyer represent the child's wishes, his best interests, as perceived by the lawyer, or both?' Perry explains it as the difference between speaking on behalf of, as opposed to speaking in place of, someone else, in this case, the child. If one is speaking on behalf of someone else, one is interpreting and representing that person – if one is speaking in place of someone else, one is simply a mouth-piece for that person – one may or may not share the views being expressed, one is simply a vehicle for the expression of the views. To speak on behalf of someone else implies a greater involvement, control over what is said, and investment in the outcome resulting from what has been said.

The Children Act, will clarify the position regarding the guardian ad litem as an independent agent. But the guardian ad litem becomes involved only when care proceedings have been initiated by the local authority. These situations concern only a small minority of the child protection case load of any given social services department. When we consider the situation of 'the child as client' we are looking at the majority of the child protection case load. In the social work client relationship, social workers generally speak 'on behalf of' clients, (whether children or adults), whereas lawyers may speak in place of or on behalf of the clients. What problems does this present to Canadian lawyers in child welfare/child protection cases? Perry's comments on this are most instructive, he writes:

> 'I suggest that commensurate with the extent to which the child has the capacity both to communicate with his counsel and to make informed decisions, which means he has reasonable comprehension of the consequences, counsel should be guided as he would if he were acting for an adult client, by the child's instructions.'

Perry observes that the primary condition is that the client is able to communicate with his counsel. The lawyer will inform the client about the various legal and other circumstances, interpret the law to the client and give his opinion as to the likely outcome of a particular course of action. The lawyer will, in effect, try to influence and persuade the client along certain lines but, as Perry points out, this is how lawyers normally carry out their work. He argues that with respect to child clients it need not be different, provided only that the young client is able to communicate with their representative, the lawyer, and to comprehend consequences. Clearly this rules out infants and those unable to communicate meaningfully. Other safeguards are required to address those problems.

The problem for the social worker of seeing the child as client is more complex than that which lawyers face in similar circumstances. In essence the status of the social work client is in itself different from the lawyer's client, though they are both called 'clients'. Traditionally users of social work services have been classified as 'clients' and that term has come to be associated with dependency and need. So for children to become social worker clients, as traditionally understood, may simply reinforce their position of dependency and need. However, there is nothing mandatory about this, and it may well be that the 'new consumerism' hanging about the welfare services could change this. What are the risks of social workers treating young people as serious users of their services and speaking 'in their place' rather than on their behalf? These issues require further review.

The first problem is to do with the child/young person's capacity to give an informed view and to comprehend the consequences. Where the child/young person is too young, or has a severe learning impairment, there is no choice but that the State takes over and appoints someone to give instructions for the child. In cases other than these the social worker who is involved in CPW must treat the child as the client and should define the term 'client' to ensure that the young person is, as far as possible, an active person. The professional view of children as victims of child abuse, including sexual abuse, also adds to the problem of defining and treating the child as the client. The received wisdom in social work is that the experience of being a victim results in guilt and low self-esteem; where the abuse has occurred within the family, the child often wishes to keep the family together and may subsequently retract statements. This may lead some social workers to view some child clients as unreliable.

In these circumstances what else can social workers do? The risks would appear to be evenly balanced and social workers will lose either way. Therefore, there is no option but to accept what the client says and, if the social work view is different, to present that as an alternative explanation, both to the client and to other interested parties. It was Sarte who said 'in the end you have to believe what people tell you, anything else is tyranny'. Some children who were caught up in the Cleveland affair felt that they were not believed and all their efforts to put their cases were simply interpreted as attempts to hide the truth and to protect the guilty. The problem with this scenario is that it leaves the social worker as the sole arbiter of 'the truth' and, since it is likely that they already have some precon- ceived ideas, this is a dangerous position in which to be. It is not in the interest of social workers, clients or society for them to occupy such a position.

Within the law social workers do their best to offer children the opportunity to end their oppression and abuse. Such offers of help must be based on professional judgement and the use of their skills and knowledge. Ultimately social workers have to accept that their young clients may make decisions or choices which appear not to be in their own best interest. This is no different from clients in other situations such as women who go back to brutal partners and have 'wasted' social work time. The young client may base her/his decision on factors which the social worker can only guess at. It is difficult to weigh the cost of one set of actions/outcomes as against another, when all seem equally dismal and hopeless. The important thing is that the young person knows that the Child Protection Service is available and what it does, and has confidence to approach the social worker for assistance when they feel able or willing to seek help. It is really about accepting the limits to professional intervention and working within these limits.

There are times when this would not apply – but it is not simply a matter of the child's view as against the social worker's. It should be more a matter of the weight of evidence and where it points. Where the social worker is convinced that harm is being done to a child, it is not simply a question of taking the child's word or not, but of being guided by a complete assessment based on all available evidence. The new legislation should provide social workers with a clearer indication of what constitutes 'assessment' in CPW. Any 'evidence' would necessarily include the social workers' own professional observations and views. If the evidence does not support the child's view, these views may have to be set aside in order to protect the child from further harm or to avoid their being harmed. The decision should not rest on a view that the child's opinions, wishes and attitudes towards what has occurred should be disregarded simply because s/he is a child. In much the same way as, under relevant Mental Health legislation, an adult's views may be set aside to protect the patient or the public. The fact that there are times when a client's views are to be disregarded should not have implications for the generality of clients. These occurrences should be the exception rather than the rule. In the final analysis – who is to say whether its better to stay among people one knows and be abused or be placed among strangers and run the risk of further abuse? It is also essential that the young client be properly informed of their rights and of their status as clients. This information should be conveyed in a written form and in language which is easily understood by children and young people.

The matter of confidentiality is also of concern in relation to information which a child or young person discloses to a social worker. If a child makes an allegation against someone, but the information has been given on condition that it is kept secret – where does that leave the social worker? The social worker should not give a promise of secrecy; the information may have far reaching implications, for instance for the local authority's placement policy affecting all children in its care. Lord Justice Butler-Sloss, in a case where a social worker had withheld allegations of abuse from foster-parents, because of an undertaking given to the child, stated that:

> 'A serious allegation cannot be ignored and probably will eventually have to be revealed to the police, doctors and others. A child cannot be sheltered from the conse-quences of the information disclosed and should be told truthfully of the likely outcome . . . . . . any other approach is unjust to the child and to the adults con-cerned.' The Guardian, Law Report 14.07.89

Children all over the world are exposed to abuse of various kinds, either from their own parents and other adults, or as a consequence of national and international politics. Social workers as professionals engaged in front-line child protection work have to try their hardest to ensure that they do not in any way add to the oppression and exploitation of children. One possible way towards achieving this end is to begin to both define and treat the child as the client. They should see the status of clients in more equal and active terms and compromise this only when careful and systematic assessment indicates the necessity for a different course of action. It is funda-mental to this approach that the social status of 'child' and/or 'client' is not used to marginalise and disregard the views and wishes of those most affected by social work intervention. Social workers must respond to allegations of abuse from children in residential and foster care, in the same way as they do to allegations of parental abuse, and not dismiss them as 'part of the child's problem'.

The anticipated response to many of the views expressed here will be that the law already provides for children's views and wishes to be taken into account. In practice, the implementation of laws and procedures are influenced by a number of factors: the values and attitudes of the professionals, resource allocation, management and supervision are probably of equal importance. There are many areas of discretionary decision-making, which allow the personal and professional views of adults – lawyers, social workers and doctors – to have a major influence on the outcome. The values which are attached to the social status both of 'children' and 'clients' means that unless the view of clients changes, the position of children would not really improve by simply calling them 'clients'. The situation requires a more fundamental change in the perception of the role and status of both groups. In order to overcome the difficulties of viewing and treating the child as the client, it might be helpful to come to some understanding of what the difficulties are and to what they relate. It is also important that the child does not compete with others for the status of client. In the Beckford report (1985), the Committee of Inquiry commented on the need for social workers in child protection work to treat the child as 'the primary' client.

This does not go far enough, it sets up a hierarchy of 'clients', starting with the child as the primary client. Given the problems which social workers experience in targeting and focusing their work, it is unlikely that a hierarchy would work. On the contrary, it might actually weaken the child's position. Children as 'primary clients' will compete with adults as 'secondary clients' for social work attention, with predictable results. A child protection service must focus primarily and exclusively on children, other services must be developed to respond to the very different problems of abusers. It is not feasible for the same service and the same workers to protect children *and* to work with offenders. That is an impossible task which social workers in CPW would do well to question and reject.

There are practical implications to viewing the child as *the* client: these are to do with the victim's right to take independent legal action and to seek compensation. Victims, including those abused in the family can apply to the Criminal Injuries Compensation Board for compensation. There are time limits to these claims and compensation cannot be awarded to a person who is living in the same house as the offender. Social workers should bear this in mind when looking at placement options. Proposed reforms to the legal system mean that children will soon have access to legal aid. Social workers should actively encourage children and young people to get legal advice in their own right and to seek compensation for their injuries. Compensation can never undo the harm, but it may give some the means to stop being homeless, who would deny them that?

Child Protection Work – Defining the Task

Having considered the matter of the child as the client in child protection work, we now turn to examine what that work primarily involves in terms of tasks, roles and functions. An earlier section explained the background against which CPW developed in the UK. It was pointed out that although historically child abuse has taken many forms, the focus of social work intervention has been on the family. It was suggested that this partial understanding of the problem has led to a partial response, which in itself may be damaging to the child victim. In seeking to define the role, tasks and functions of social workers in CPW, we will examine the way this work is conceptualised and practiced and will point out limitations inherent in the current model.

Child protection work as currently practiced in Britain is located within the local authority statutory Social Services Departments (in Scotland, Social Work Departments). The local authority SSDs undertake 95% of all protection work, with the NSPCC undertaking the remaining 5% (ADSS Survey, 1989). The relationship between SSDs and local NSPCC offices vary, but tensions do exist and problems can develop. Following the Beckford inquiry there was quite a lot of fear among local authority social workers that child protection work would be taken away from them and given to the NSPCC. As things stand, local authorities are responsible through the Social Services Committee and the Director of Social Services, for almost all statutory child care. In Britain the structure of local and central government is such that the central government, in this case the Department of Health, under the relevant Minister, retains overall responsibility for the Child Protection Service.

In order to arrive at some understanding of what any job of work involves it is usual to carry out a job analysis; a job analysis identifies the content of the work, the different levels at which it is performed and the skills and knowledge required to carry it out competently. The nature of CPW makes a job analysis exercise particularly relevant. Goldberg (1979) described attempts to develop a 'case review system' in an SSD and the difficulties social workers experienced in evaluating their work. Social workers preferred to define their interventions in vague terms (e.g. 'casework' or 'review visiting') and found it difficult to state precise aims, or to identify exactly what they were trying to achieve in any particular instance. These problems suggest that the use of some of the tools of job analysis may be helpful to social workers. These tools, being specific, systematic and 'objective', may help in ways which open ended methods do not. The inherent difficulties and problems of the work will not diminish or disappear simply as a result of using semi-technical language to describe them.

A job analysis should: (a) provide a definition of the purpose and objectives of the job; (b) provide a description of the roles which go with the job; (c) identify the tasks, functions which go with each role; (d) locate the job within the overall management and organisational framework; and (e) identify criteria on which to base a programme of personal and professional development, training, supervision and support, and future appraisals.

Social workers must get to grips with the language of the workplace by which their performance will be assessed, otherwise they will find themselves at a great disadvantage. Whether or not this language is appropriate for the task is not the point; in order to discuss the matter, one has to be familiar with it. But the approach taken here is that such language is useful, especially in contrast to the often vague, all-embracing and woolly language of social work. If it is a job of work that's being analysed, it makes sense to use the tools of job analysis which have been found useful elsewhere. Provided that the limitations of these tools are identified and accepted, they should be valid when applied to CPW.

The areas identified as essential to a job analysis exercise have been listed as being:

1) Definition of purpose and objectives.

2) Description of roles association with the job.

3) Identification of the associated tasks and functions.

4) Location of the job within overall management and organisational context.

5) Identification of indicators from which to develop a programme of personal and professional development, training, supervision and support; and against which to appraise future work.

The DHSS (1986) categorized Child Abuse under these five headings:

1) *Physical injury* Any form of injury including deliberate poisoning, where there is a definite knowledge, or a reasonable suspicion that, the injury was inflicted, or knowingly not prevented, by any person having custody of the child.

2) *Neglect* The persistent or severe neglect of a child (for example, by exposure to any kind of danger including cold and starvation) which results in serious impairment of the child's health and development.

3) *Emotional ill-treatment* The severe adverse effect upon emotional development caused either by persistent or severe neglect or rejection, on the part of the parent or carer.

4) *Sexual abuse* The involvement of dependent, developmentally immature children and adolescents in sexual activities they do not comprehend, to which they are unable to give informed consent, violate the social taboos of family roles, or are against the law.

5) *Potential abuse* Children in situations where they have not been abused but where social and medical assessments indicate a high degree of risk that they might be abused in the future, including situations where another child in the household has been harmed, or the household contains a known abuser.

The framework below is an attempt to analyse the nature and content of CPW. Social workers as agents of the local authority social services departments are expected to carry out these functions on behalf of the local authority and of society. The purpose and objectives of the service is to protect children in circumstances where the family and the community have failed them.

Child Protection Work – Job Analysis

Role	Tasks/Functions	Organisation Management
Policing	investigation and surveillance. Check and monitor; present evidence	supervised by and responsible to line-manager or CPW specialist
Legal and Procedural	carrying out tasks as stated in law, implementing procedures liaising with other agencies, calling Case Conferences etc	Area Review Committees LA Legal Dept DoH, Social Work Advisers etc
Professional and Welfare	making assessments developing a CP Plan implementing the Child Protection Plan	Child Protection specialist training: in-house and external
Administrative	keeping full accurate and appropriate records in all the above areas of work.	Managing and Admin Officer; training department

Social workers in CPW are encouraged to analyse their work in terms of these parameters and to try to conceptualise this work in ways which enable proper analysis of tasks and functions. This provides a proper focus to the work and enables the job to been seen for what it is, a job of work. It also means that social workers equipped with such understanding are better placed, both to carry out the work and to defend themselves if things go wrong – as unfortunately, they will.

Child protection work contains a very strong investigative element, involving the actual policing of communities and families. This creates problems and conflict for people who were primarily attracted to social work in order to 'help' people. Their understanding of social work and of themselves as professionals in this field, does not include these aspects which are generally at odds with their philosophy and values. In connection with the job content of CPW it is important to note that some of these features are unique to CPW. As child protection work has expanded so too has its impact on the job profile and content of social work. To illustrate this point – on 13 June, 1989 Central Television News ran an item on sexual abuse of children in the East Midlands. The news item said that resulting from an earlier case which the police believed had been cleared up, but which the social workers felt had not; an 'undercover unit' of social workers had continued its investigations and had accumulated evidence to show that the police had definitely underestimated the nature and extent of child sexual abuse.

The content of the news item left viewers in little doubt that the social workers had acted literally as police or detectives in tracking down suspects and monitoring their movements, in order to establish their guilt, or at least to prove that they had a case to answer. Time was when social workers were defensive about being described as 'soft cops', meaning that as agents of social control they policed the poor. The scale and nature of child abuse has changed all that in relation to child protection work; but not everyone is happy about or willing to accept this degree of change nor such an overt investigative and policing role for social workers. In the field of child protection, feelings can be very strong, this is a normal human reaction to the work. But the structures within which social workers operate should harness these feelings to constructive ends. Questions must be asked about the role and competence of social workers as detectives, about the training and resource implications of undertaking such work and the implications for colleagues from other agencies. (This, of course, assumes that the TV news report was correct in every detail).

Practitioners who are unhappy with such developments should not be timid about raising their concerns in a helpful way. They should insist on a proper explanation of the reasons why social workers should undertake such work themselves, about training for it and about any necessary safeguards. Social workers should not allow their professional profile and the content of the work they do to be radically changed by default. Child protection work, in terms of the quality of the direct service, will not be improved by social workers becoming detectives. It is best to use all means available to encourage the police to do the detective work.

Child protection work has brought many challenges to social workers, putting old problems (e.g. who is the client?) in a different context and posing some new ones. At times the scale of these problems threatens to overwhelm both individuals and agencies. It is not surprising therefore that a response has sometimes been lacking and that developments have been somewhat *ad hoc*. Some developments are of such a profound nature that they may well change the professional and job profile of social work completely. This chapter has attempted to identify and discuss some of the issues, and to suggest constructive responses to some of the challenges raised in the practice of child protection work.

Summary of the Main Points
This chapter concerned itself with two main objectives – (a) defining the client, and (b) defining the task.

1) The child was presented as the client of the child protection service.

2) Problems and issues associated with the definition of the child as the client were identified and discussed.

3) It was argued that the term 'client' as used in social work may not, when applied to children, greatly enhance their status, and their chances of being taken seriously.

4) It was suggested that the term 'client' as applied to CPW must have a more active and participatory meaning.

5) It was argued that in cases where children are unable, for whatever reason, to function as clients, other independent provision must be made to protect the child's interest.

6) It was suggested that social workers should accept limits to their intervention, consistent with good practice.

7) Child protection work as a professional social work activity was analysed in terms of its roles/tasks/functions, and the changes which the profession is undergoing in response to the scale and nature of child abuse in society.

The analysis offered in this chapter is intended to deepen practitioners understanding of some of the underlying issues, and to provide a more informed basis for the practice of social work in this field.

Introduction
Part Two

The remaining three chapters of this book present an analysis of the contextual, professional and personal challenges facing social workers in carrying out their child protection work. The purpose is, as with the rest of the book, to help practitioners to develop adequate and helpful responses to the problems they are facing. Each chapter in this section includes suggestions for action and response but, in common with the rest of the book, the hope is that these suggestions will trigger and promote new action and responses as part of an on-going process of change and development.

This part of the book draws on research, direct work and many years of teaching consultancy and supervision in social work. Inevitably some people will find the approach to some subjects disturbing or even distasteful. No apologies are offered. Social workers are in the business of encouraging or even forcing others to confront difficult, painful and distressing matters. They should not complain when the same is expected of them. Survival techniques and coping strategies are useful only if based on an honest discussion of the issues. The issues and problems must be fully analysed and suggestions for action must acknowledge the human weaknesses which all people share.

The author has drawn extensively from her own personal and professional experience in writing the whole of this book, but especially so in this section. This personal and professional experience includes being a black woman academic/professional in a predominantly white male academic world – with all that this implies. The experience of being born and brought up in one culture (Barbadian), going to college in another (Indian), and living, working and bringing up a family in yet another (British) has certainly been very enriching. Social work practice, teaching and supervision enabled wide exposure to different parts of Britain – from the rural South West to inner city London. Research and consultancy work with professionals in education and youth work, has extended and deepened my knowledge and understanding of people-centred work; and, of course, being a mother brought its own riches of pleasure and pain and put another perspective on the experience of schools and 'adolescent problems'. Becoming a grand-mother has added yet another perspective.

All these experiences contribute to one's views and understanding of the world and the problems of human existence which we all face and try to deal with. An example of how things interact is provided by the following anecdote. During the fieldwork on the research study of *Social Work Training for Child Protection Work*, (Stone, 1988), I was told by one of the female social work practitioners, during a telephone interview, that women get a lot of sexual pleasure from looking after young children, 'We have access to their private parts – nappy changing, bathing brings us into contact with children's genitals . . . . .' As it happened I was looking after my ten month old grandson during that time; as I changed the next dirty nappy I couldn't help thinking that if there were people who did enjoy this, then they were welcome to it! I can change nappies with the best of them – but to equate it with sexual pleasure, or to say one enjoys it (other than in the sense of a job well done and a less smelly baby) seems to me utter nonsense. I changed my first nappy, or diaper as we call it in Barbados, when I was 11 years old, so I think I can claim some experience in this field.

As a woman academic and as a mother I thought about that female social worker's observation with some concern. It seemed to me impossible to change a dirty nappy without touching a baby's private parts. It seemed ironic and unjust to accuse women (who in changing nappies at least – are literally doing the dirty work of looking after children) of misusing this role to gain sexual gratifica-tion. It was particularly interesting to have such a view expressed by a woman, who was also a mother of young children. It is a strange world, and the possibility of some people gaining satisfaction in this way cannot be entirely discounted, but it is hard to accept this as an observation on the general relationship between women and young children.

The mixture of personal and professional experience has enabled me to write with an approach to issues which is not only original and helpful, but also I hope, challenging and provocative.

Inevitably, writing this book has involved me in a reflective process with regard to my own professional experience of this work. This has brought back many things, including my fairly traumatic reactions to being told by my supervisor that a child I'd admired was 'not bad for an incest baby'. Twenty years later, as I listened to social workers talking about their feelings and reactions to the work, I knew exactly what they were talking about. The difference was that, twenty years on, it was acceptable to talk about these matters, research was being done, training and support is available and, books like this are being written.

In the late 1960s, as a student (of Social Administration) I was attached to the Moral Welfare Worker in an area of South London and more or less shadowed her for two days a week. Every Wednesday we went to the local police station for a meeting with the male Sergeant and the female Police Constable who made up the police arm of the moral welfare establishment. These meetings covered the release from custody of the local paedophiles, the latest on the houses where child sex rings were suspected of operating, reports from local teachers of suspected abuse and other matters of this sort. The rest of the Moral Welfare Worker's job consisted of visiting schoolgirl mothers and pregnant school girls often the result of incest by step-father or, less frequently, by natural fathers. This was at a time when many teenage children were being brought over from the Caribbean to join new families: fathers and mothers they had not seen since early childhood, and quite often step-fathers they had never seen before. A number of girls in these families turned up in the Moral Welfare Worker's case load. I was deeply touched by the plight of all the young women on the MWW's case load but the black girls had a profoundly disturbing effect on me. Their situation was compounded by the racism which was all around us and which would inevitably worsen an already blighted young life. Some of these schoolgirl mothers were as young as twelve or thirteen, one or two still clung to their dolls. These are some of the experiences which makes it impossible for me to see organisational flow charts and checklists as the answer to the emotional and psychological effects of this work. However, I know that they can be an aid, promote clarity and maintain a focus, so that emotional and psychological reactions do not overwhelm or distract workers.

It is important that practitioners understand the underlying issues so that they do not add to problems. Any analysis of the role of the social worker in relation to CPW must acknowledge the organisational and structural constraints on practitioners, the limitations of inadequate training and staff support, and the nature of the work itself. The absence of a theory which offers an adequate explanation of child abuse and thus provides a sound basis for practice, is a central issue. These factors have implications for the adequacy of the social work response; it is not just the skills and competencies of the individual worker which are decisive to the outcome of the intervention.

Each of the remaining chapters deals with a set of critical factors which influence the practice of CPW. Some issues, such as gender, race and class are central and surface in each chapter, the implications of each depend on the context. Chapter 3 examines the 'Contextual' issues: structural arrangements, law, inter-agency work etc. Chapter 4 deals with 'Professional' matters – including management, supervision, training and the implications of the theory deficit for practice. Chapter 5 returns to some of the areas already covered, but looks ·at them from a different 'Personal' angle. New areas – those affecting practitioners lives are also explored. Chapter 6 contains some concluding comments.

Chapter 3
Focus on the Contextual Dimension of Child Protection Work

In 1974 Brunel University produced an analysis of SSD's, examining their 'developing patterns of work and organisation'. The authors examined the status of professional social workers in these departments and concluded that they were not 'autonomous professionals'. They suggested that social workers were operating within what they termed a structure of 'delegated discretion'; and commented that although:

> 'the situation of genuine professional autonomy is neither unknown in practise, nor unthinkable in social work in particular. However it must be recorded that virtually all staff . . . of whatever grade with whom we have seriously discussed this issue, unhesitatingly concluded . . . . that the situation of social workers in SSDs is one of exercising delegated discretion rather than professional autonomy, and is likely to remain so . . . . . . it is universally accepted that present-day Directors of departments are accountable to their employing authorities for all the work done within departments and for how it is done.' (P.100)

Their location within the local authority structure presents social workers as a professional group with many challenges and problems. In the field of CPW these problems take on particular forms, both because of the nature of the work itself and because of the organisational framework of the Social Services Department, and its place within the local authority structure. In particular, social workers lack any degree of autonomy in their decision making, which puts them at odds with the claim to be professionals (and is probably the first cause of potential problems and conflicts for many new recruits to social work.) At the same time this very lack of autonomy offers a degree of protection – or should do. This is the other side of the coin which many social workers often fail to appreciate and use to their advantage. Location within the local authority means that social workers do not and cannot operate as independent practitioners. However, the exercise of 'delegated discretion' within a system of professional supervision and management relationships which ensure effective monitoring and accountability, should enable social workers to offer a professional standard of service.

The Brunel University research identified a lack of organisational clarity as one of the central weaknesses of local authority social services departments. This lack of organisational clarity has important implications for the practice and management of social work and CPW in particular. Among the most pressing problems which this presents to the practitioner is the competing interests and needs of different client groups, and the allocation of scarce resources within these groups. This 'gate-keeping' function, which is essentially related to keeping the organisation functioning, in the first instance falls heavily on practitioners. The high profile given to CPW and the lack of organisational clarity in terms of priorities, objectives, aims and goals, means that all CPW automatically gets an immediate response. The question of professional judgement or the interests of other client groups just does not come into it.

Social workers within the local authority social services departments are worried and concerned about the possible 'privatisation' of the local authority child care and child protection functions. Or, if not privatisation, then at least the hiving off of these services to specialist voluntary organisations – in particular the NSPCC. The level of anxiety is so high that social workers are beginning to be defensive about the involvement of the voluntary sector in any statutory child care provision, holding to the view that the state must take primary and often total responsibility for such provision (Stone, 1989). This possibility of the social services losing their statutory child care role presents social workers, already under siege, with a further cause for anxiety and another source of insecurity about their role and purpose. At the same time, such proposals confirm the view that social services departments, as presently organised, are not offering a good service generally and, in particular, not a good child protection service.

A further implication of the way social services are organised and delivered relates to access to such scarce resources as day care facilities, and the means whereby poor, usually single parent families, gain such access. It has been suggested (Grima-Asrat, 1989) that young single black mothers do try 'to work the system' in order to gain access to day care. They do this by saying that they are at risk of abusing their children. This is the only sure way of getting a place at a local authority day nursery. What is the social work practitioner to do in a situation where she suspects this to be the case? It is possible to treat such an application lightly, to dismiss it as an attempt at 'playing the system', but how are such cases to be identified? As long as access to such scarce resources are tightly controlled, people will continue to try to beat the system and some will undoubtedly get caught at it. An immediate, helpful and practical response would be to educate and inform people about the role and purpose of social services departments and about procedures relating to CPW. At the most basic level, such 'education' might consist of a brochure, containing basic information on the role and function of the social services department and its powers, in relation to children experiencing or at risk of abuse. The production of a leaflet of this kind should be well within the budget of each local authority, or maybe the Department of Health would be best suited to producing this type of information for the population at large.

This brief analysis of social services departments, presents a picture of an organisation unclear about its own role and purpose, with scarce resources, the rationing of which falls mainly on the direct workers. In the field of CPW these factors can lead to several anomalies: it adds to the already high degree of stress, forcing hard pressed social workers to make impossible decisions about allocating scarce resources; it co-opts into the system people who are attempting to use that system to their own advantage but who may misjudge the nature of that system and become trapped within it. This competition for scarce resources and the emergence of an artificially created client group, creates particular problems and adds to the tensions within the already highly charged and demanding field of CPW.

Inter-Agency Work

The problems of inter-agency work in child protection are focused, for many social workers, on the Case Conference and Case Conference procedures. The main areas of concern for many social workers can be summarised as follows:

1) The potential for conflict with other professionals whose values and attitudes may be different.

2) The procedures guiding inter-agency work, which although accepted as necessary, suffer from problems of interpretation, emphasis and discretionary decision-making in practice.

3) Presentational problems – how to present arguments, evidence, hunches, 'gut feelings' beliefs, information, in a convincing, and professional manner.

4) Problems in using research findings, and insights from the professional literature, without sounding too academic, and putting people off.

5) How to avoid being put down by other professionals, especially medics, in the case conference setting.

6) How to maintain confidentiality, whilst at the same time following the procedures, and protecting children.

One thing which strikes anyone who has observed Case Conferences at work is the informal, unprepared approach which often characterizes the social work contribution. This makes it very easy for others, who are perhaps better organised and better prepared, to score points over them, or to not take the social workers contribution as seriously as perhaps they should. Where these complaints are legitimate social workers have to take responsibility for their failure to convince fellow-professionals. It has been suggested, for example, that Magistrates are more likely to follow the recommendations of school reports (on children appearing before the juvenile court), than social workers' Social Inquiry Reports, because school reports use everyday English, and the spelling is better. Millham (1981) compared magistrates' reactions to teachers reports *vis à vis* social work reports:

> 'The school report carries greater weight with magistrates than the social work reports, because it is written in a language they understand, is spelt correctly and is rather less justifying in its analysis of the child's behaviour.'

Although the implied criticism of social workers for being rather too 'justifying' of the child's behaviour could be debated, there is a serious point there about bad presentation, obscure language and poor spelling. Social workers should not be too dismissive of such comments, especially in the context of inter-agency work. Many social work colleagues who are very professional in their own approach, are often appalled and embarrassed by some of their colleagues more amateurish approaches. So there is definitely a case to answer and social workers and their managers must accept that preparation is essential in this context.

Thorough preparation is essential. Those not used to making presentations may find the following tips helpful: to begin with design a presentation format (and go through this with a supervisor or colleague). If you are daunted by the task of referring to or using research/professional literature, then it might be helpful to abstract a few notes, highlight any salient points and circulate them beforehand. If this is not possible, take them with you, speak briefly about them and then hand them out. You may find this a bit difficult the first few times, but you'll soon get use to it. Such inputs increase the body of common knowledge shared by the Case Conference members, which builds up over time and contributes towards the quality of their decision making both as a group and individually.

Inter-agency work brings professionals with very different values, perceptions and work conditions together; procedures often appear to ignore these differences, or assume that they will somehow be accommodated. As the response to child abuse grows, and more and more professionals are co-opted into the field, it is as well to consider some of these issues and problems. CPW brings social workers, Headteachers and classroom teachers into close contact. But social workers normally work in people's homes whereas schools are public institutions. Teachers in the classroom have problems of maintaining order, control and their status as teachers, which by-and-large do not trouble social workers. Anybody who has worked in a school knows how difficult it is to stop gossip and rumour; this is especially true about sexual abuse and incest. Children's lives become impossible, particularly when everyone in the staff room, and possibly the playground, knows that a child has been sexually abused. 'A girl in my school was sexually abused by both her parents. The social workers came to the school, and there was lots of meetings and things . . . . . everyone got to know . . . . . her life was hell, everyone knew . . . . . her whole life was destroyed she tried to kill herself because she just couldn't stand it no more, it was really, really bad . . . . .' (Comments of a 17 year old London girl during a research interview with the author, Stone, 1989).

As the response to all types of child abuse grows, and the Department of Health guidelines begin to take effect, it is important for the adults involved to consider children as people and not make things any worse for them. The intentions behind inter-agency work are very good, but no infra-structure of training and support exists to help these intentions to be realised. This means that social workers have to adopt strategies to help both themselves, and their colleagues in other agencies, to deliver the best child protection service possible.

Law and Criminal Justice
Many social workers find it extremely difficult to work with the criminal justice system, the police, the courts and the prison system. The obvious exception here is the Probation Service which is staffed by social workers who specialise and offer a specialist service to the courts. In the matter of child protection, some social workers have in the past been very reluctant to involve the police and to work with

them. In recent years this has changed, as social work practice in this field has itself come to resemble many aspects of police work. This has coincided with the development of joint training schemes for Police Officers and social workers by several Social Services Departments and Police Authorities.

Even so, some tensions remain, and these are centred for many on:

1) The social workers' understanding of the causes of child abuse.

2) Their corresponding perceptions that these causes are not remedied by putting offenders in prisons.

3) The knowledge that prisons have not proved effective in deterring other offenders, or in preventing other types of crimes.

4) The belief that the law and the criminal justice system, is by and large the wrong response to the question of child abuse.

5) The investigation and criminalisation of people, whatever wrong they have done, is not a motivation for becoming a social worker; and is at odds with social work values which emphasise the capacity of human beings for growth, learning and change.

Whilst the basis of these concerns can be understood, the law remains the principal means by which citizens secure justice. The fact that the criminal justice system is itself imperfect should not be a reason to treat offenders who abuse and injure children differently from others. Although some offenses are 'child specific', as, for example, having sex with a girl under sixteen, most offenses against children are not status offenses; rape and sexual assault are serious criminal offenses whatever the age of the victim. Some people have argued that the term 'child abuse' is not a useful term, that it 'cleans-up' dreadful crimes against children and that the terminology itself should express the exact nature of the crimes committed.

Social workers perceive the causes of the physical abuse and neglect of children as being primarily related to social and environmental factors, interacting with the personality of the abuser and the abused. Physical abuse and neglect are seen as particularly closely related to class and social deprivation; whereas sexual abuse can occur across the spectrum. A later section will look more closely at social class and examine some assumptions about the relationship of poverty and social deprivation to child abuse. But it is clear that if social workers' perceptions about the origins of at least a proportion of child abuse is correct, then they are right in thinking that the law and the criminal justice system would not provide an adequate response in terms of the causation and are unlikely, therefore, to have any impact in terms of protecting children from future abuse.

The use of the law and the criminal justice system in this context is seen as purely punitive; and this causes many problems and anxieties for social workers.

The question of punishment is a difficult one, but it seems fair to say that if that is how the law of the land operates, social workers should not seek to undermine it. It is also the case that the non-punishment treatment approaches to offenders are difficult to apply, and not markedly more successful in their impact. Recent disclosures of the way that sex offenders use groupwork and other therapeutic techniques to manipulate female probation officers and other prison staff, attest to the dangers and limitations of this approach. (*The Independent*, 13 September, 1989). Abusive behaviour appear to be highly addictive and it seems that approaches based on treatment regimes designed for addicts may be more appropriate for this type of offender.

Social Class and Social Deprivation

A recent case in America exposed extreme abuse in a middle-class white American family, where the man regularly and systematically used violence to control and oppress his wife and daughter. In the end he killed his six year old daughter. This case has received a lot of publicity in America, where it was televised live as it unfolded in court, and in Britain where it was widely reported both for its newsworthiness and in connection with a proposal to televise court proceedings in the UK. (*Eye Witness*, BBC 1, June 8, 1989) A very interesting aspect of this case was the reaction of surprise and astonishment at the picture of white middle class American family life which unfolded in the course of the court case. Commentators were amazed at the brutality, cruelty, drug taking etc which went on in families pretty much like their own. But one group of people were not surprised, the armies of black American and Caribbean women who service the needs of white middle class American families – they were not surprised. For an interesting, though fictional account of middle class white American family life which included systematic child abuse, which the black housekeeper knew of but dared not speak about, see Toni Morrison's novel *Tar Baby*.

The middle classes are relatively protected from the vigilance of the state welfare bureaucracy. Working class people on the whole are more available for surveillance and poor people in particular are subjected to a degree of surveillance which is frightening in some of its aspects. The result of this is that there is an enormous amount of information covering all aspects of working class and poor people's lifestyles and very little, if any, on middle class lifestyles. Further, because most professionals are themselves middle class, they inevitably fail to see negative aspects of middle class life, or to interpret patterns of behaviour in a more positive light.

It is now time for another anecdote, this time it concerns an Adult Education Class (as it was then), in the home countries of England; the time is the mid-seventies. The class is doing an 'O' Level course in 'Family and Community Studies'. The class members are all female, all white middle class English women, except me, the tutor, who is black Afro-Caribbean. We are all in our late twenties – early thirties, from professional backgrounds and with husbands who are the same. During a session on family-life, the question of violence in the family is being dealt with, and the discussion turns to child abuse. Once the matter of child abuse was raised the discussion took on an entirely different dimension, as one by one, the women began to talk of their experiences of mothering. One woman said that she had once thrown her daughter against a wall. This revelation was prompted by something in the course material which suggested that stress brought about by poverty and social deprivation was the main cause of the physical abuse of children by parents. She disputed this, and went on to explain her own circumstances and the factors which led to her being cruel to her child. She had resented giving up her job, felt trapped at home and missed the stimulation of her work. She felt unable to talk about this to anyone, including her husband, and felt she would be seen as a bad mother once her feelings were known. The incident occurred when the baby kept crying non-stop and would not respond to attempts to comfort her. The mother in telling the story, some years later, said that fortunately the baby did not receive any permanent injury, 'and the next day I applied for my old job back, and got it.'

She had been able to realise that she had been responding to unrealistic ideas of what a good mother was and, in so doing, had run the risk of permanently injuring her child. Once this had happened, she immediately changed her situation, began to enjoy her child more and a similar situation had never arisen again. Once this women had spoken, it opened the floodgates to more 'true confessions', and almost everyone in the group had a story to tell, some much worse than the first. Indeed, one was a particularly dramatic account of a life and death incident which forced the class to take an early coffee break. This mother, a qualified nursery nurse, had beaten her child, as she said 'literally, to within an inch of her life'. The child had been provoking her for hours and she'd employed all her mothering and professional skills to no avail. In the end, she snapped and started hitting the child; by the time she had stopped, the child was lying, apparently unconscious on the floor. The mother picked her up, put her in the push chair and ran with her to the doctor's surgery. When they arrived 'the little madam got up and walked' into the surgery. Even at that distance in time the mother could not recount the events without great emotion and explained the child's recovery as nothing short of a miracle. From that day, she never hit that child or any of the other children she subsequently gave birth to. An interesting feature of that story was the doctor's reaction; without hearing or asking for precise details of what had happened, he simply said that all parents hit their children sometimes.

One final anecdote concerns a female musician who found her twin sons too noisy and that the noise interfered with her practice. Each morning after her husband left for work she locked the boys in the car in the garage and they stayed there until their father returned at around 5.30pm in the evening. This went on until they were two years old, when they started at nursery. At that age, they were literally 'finding their feet', being very unsteady in standing up and unable to walk properly. During the time they were regularly locked in the garage, people in the adjoining houses could hear them crying, and once one of the neighbours tried to intervene but she was rebuffed and more or less told to mind her own business. Which she did. The boys appeared to progress normally once they started school, and are now grown men. Maybe it's best that no action was taken – who can say? But in the context of a discussion about class and the social control of families, it is worth noting that it was easy enough for this middle class mother to get away with behaviour which, in a working class neighbourhood, would have brought 'the welfare round' in no time at all. These examples, both of serious physical assaults on children, help to demonstrate how some of the conditions, unrelated to social class but very much related to stress and women's circumstances, lead to children being physically abused. They also help to show how middle class people are protected from surveillance. In the second case, if that had been a working class mother, almost certainly the doctor would have asked the social worker or health visitor to call and check on the mother and child. But the middle class mothers get away with being told 'not to worry'.

In relation to sexual abuse, middle class children are at risk from within the family and possibly at greater risk of abuse from outside the family. The recent cases involving headmasters and teachers in private boarding schools charged with grave sexual offences against children in their care shows the risks attached to middle class life styles. But because child pornography and paedophilia appears to be linked to affluence as much as to anything else, we can expect to see the children of the middle classes being equally affected by this. We shall have to wait to see whether society will respond in the same way when predominantly working class children are involved. Middle class children may be cared for by au pairs, mothers' helps, nannies etc, all of whom may bring the child into contact with other people. Such contacts carry risk, and these risks are attached to particular life styles – just as being working class or poor, or both, also carries particular risks.

It might be helpful to illustrate the risks of sexual abuse which middle class children face with a couple of examples drawn from confidential information made available to the writer. In the first case a professional, middle-aged mother of three children was told by her daughter, (20 years old at the time of the 'disclosure') that she'd been sexually abused by the husband of the much-loved and valued nanny over a six year period. The abuse had occurred from age six to about age twelve. Although it appeared that sexual intercourse had not taken place, the length of time over which it had lasted and the degree of 'mind control' exercised by the man over the young child had made it impossible for her to tell her mother at the time. The family and, in particular, the mother was almost destroyed by the revelation. They were advised not to take any action since the abuse had occurred such a long time ago and no good would be served by stirring things up. The second example concerns a very similar type of family, where the eighteen year old son disclosed to his mother that an old family friend, who had been so close to the family that he was near enough a relative, had been sexually abusing him over a four year period. As the mother sought help and the investigations got underway, it came out that at least ten children, possibly more, had been involved. This is not a council estate in East London, but middle class Surrey; will this make any difference? Everything we know suggests it will.

Poverty and social deprivation have terrible consequences, both for the individuals, families and communities caught up in it, and for society at large. That is not disputed; what is disputed is that the working classes generally, and poor people in particular, are more systematically cruel to children than other social classes. Efforts to rid society of poverty and social deprivation should not be advanced on the backs of poor people – it is another case of blaming the victim. Poverty should be eliminated because it is an evil in itself. Obviously it contributes towards stress, but the direct consequences on children of being poor – inadequate diets, cold damp houses, homelessness – almost certainly damages children's physical health and ultimately their life chances much more. Social workers and others who link child abuse to social deprivation, and see a significant causal relationship between the two, are acting in good faith. They are motivated both to help the poor and to reduce child abuse, but in doing this they are stigmatising poor people even more.

In the absence of evidence on middle class and rich people's family lives, nothing much can be said about the degree and types of child abuse in those groups. An effective child protection service must recognise the limitations of existing knowledge, and the fact that existential and social problems have a differential impact on different social groups. The exact equation is unknown but such social problems as drug and alcohol abuse, pornography and family violence do affect all social classes, and contribute towards all types and varieties of child abuse. This is not an argument for not improving the lot of the poor or not striving for a more socially just and equal society. Work towards a more just and equal society must continue independent of child abuse.

Gender and Race: Social Issues and Child Protection

Gender
Gender is a central issue in child protection work. As a profession, social work remains a female dominated field at the practitioner level. At management level, in common with all forms of work, males predominate. The female frontline workers interact mainly with female clients, since males are usually unable or unwilling to be involved with 'the welfare'.

Gender issues arise also in respect of victims; are male babies more likely to be assaulted than female babies? Are adolescent girls more likely to be victims of sexual abuse than boys? Why do males figure so highly in all types of abuse? Social workers are generally concerned not to label all men as potential abusers and to accept that women can and do abuse children. But many social workers, both male and female, are uncomfortable with the gender issue, especially in relation to sexual abuse. Some male workers feel themselves demeaned as men and they feel somehow implicated and guilty. This raises problems and anxieties for those affected in this way, not least because of the unacceptability of raising and discussing such problems.

The gender issue, as it relates to women, is concerned with the changing role of women in society and the way this relates to and affects the treatment of children. Women as mothers have been blamed for all the ills of society; women are often blamed, or at least seen as partly responsible for men's actions in physically and sexually abusing children. Social workers have been way up front in alluding to 'collusive' women who tolerate their men's abuse of children. It has already been said that until women are able to exercise a degree of economic and financial independence, they will not be in a position to exercise emotional independence and choose to be free of such men. This is not an excuse for women's willingness or unwillingness to collude in child abuse, just an observation on women's social situation which may help to explain their behaviour. There is also the possibility that many women genuinely do not know that the abuse is occurring; not everyone is of a suspicious nature. Whatever the facts, it is unfair and unhelpful to put the responsibility for male behaviour on women. Where women are implicated in child abuse, as clearly they are, then they must take responsibility for that, and for the consequences.

On a social level we need to examine the relationship between men and women and women's financial and emotional dependence on men, in relation to the occurrence of child abuse. We need to provide information, advice and education on the long term effects of abuse on children so that women in these situations understand exactly what collaboration with social services means in this context. Social services departments should work with social educators in the media and elsewhere to get these basic messages across.

Race

Race is another important social issue in CPW; again we are entering an area where superficial and simple solutions to complex problems are a common feature of the social workers response. Enough has been said so far to indicate that there are serious problems in relation to social work practice and CPW. Some of these problems have been identified and discussed and their implications for child protection work considered. Particular areas will be affected by both the general problems and those specific to that area. This is very true of race; black and other minority social workers are limited, not only by the general factors which affect all social workers but by the effects of racism as well.

In the nineteen sixties, when black children were first beginning to emerge as a significant group within day care and residential institutions in Britain, several babies and young children died or became seriously ill because of failure by local authority staff and doctors to respond to their illnesses. This was because black children do not run high temperatures and also do not, in white terms, 'look ill'. The lack of a temperature was the main thing which contributed to the problem. Black children who were seriously ill would be sent to school or whatever, because they did not have a temperature. If the child was taken to the doctor, or the doctor called, only a slightly raised temperature would be found. Doctors would find nothing wrong, but eventually the child would often collapse and end up in hospital. Those days are over, but the fact that this happened is a testimony of institutional child abuse and racism.

Black communities and professionals have campaigned to raise the profile of black issues in social work. In many instances however such issues have not been fully understood and the resulting response has, if anything, added to the problems of black children. An example of this is drawn from the NSPCC Conference (1989), where Professor Stevenson proposed that black and Asian social workers should perform a specialist function in social services departments 'acting as consultants and advisers' where matters of race and culture are concerned. This is to acknowledge 'the ethnic dimension' because white social workers are afraid of working with black families. The proposal to use black social workers in this way, without ensuring that they have anything more than a common-sense appreciation of ethnic issues, seems dangerous. Personal experience will now be called in to illustrate the confusion or worse, which can result from this muddled and patronising approach, and Chapter 5 returns to this subject.

When I was a social work student, in the Student Unit where I was on placement there was a male European student. He was on full-time placement, my placement was concurrent. One day when I turned up after a three day break he appeared to be unusually friendly and somewhat persistent in his attentions. I mentioned this to one of my other colleagues and she laughed and said 'It must have been the course we had yesterday!' Further inquiries revealed that a black male social worker had led a session on 'Caribbean women and child rearing' in which he had said that Caribbean women traditionally had several male partners and several children by different fathers. My overseas colleagues had taken that as a more or less open invitation to check out black women. I tried not to react to the irony of the situation – here was this black male setting up black women – and probably doing it because he though it would help them.

I decided to find out more and, after identifying who the speaker was, I went to see him, just so he could know what effect his contribution had had on at least one member of his audience. I asked him about the session and got him to tell me how it had gone. Then I asked him about his own academic and professional background and his knowledge and experience of Caribbean history and culture. It turned out that he had left the Caribbean when he was five, had never returned, and had studied a conventional social science degree at a UK university, undertaking social work training on a post-graduate course. Not only did he lack specialist knowledge of Caribbean history and culture, he lacked exposure to that culture on any level. My understanding of his situation was that he felt unable to refuse to contribute when asked. He felt that such a refusal would be seen in a negative light, and as a black social worker, he could not miss the opportunity to 'raise black issues'. I never did tell him about my experience, I felt too sorry for him, and sympathised with him for the intolerable situation in which he'd been placed.

During this same period, while I was a social work student at the London School of Economics, the only input students were allowed to make to the course was when I and another black student (the total number of black students at that time) were asked to present a half-day session. I forget what the precise title of the session was, but I know it was to do with 'working with black families'. I profoundly disagreed with what this represented and I did not take part, but the circumstances prevented me from giving my true reasons. The students had between them considerable experience of social and community work, much more than many of the tutors. Yet in the area that we lacked any particular knowledge or skills, two of us were called on to 'make a contribution', on no other basis than that we were black. My colleague took a different view from me and she went ahead with the session. There is not the time or space to deal with these matters fully, but white readers should ask themselves when was the last time they were asked to perform a professional task on no other basis than their whiteness?

Examples abound of social services departments interpreting 'the ethnic dimension' in social work, to mean creating a second rate service for black children and families. The implications for the safety of black children experiencing or at risk of abuse, are very serious. The racial issues underlying the Jasmine Beckford case were never fully and honestly explored, there were too many vested interests. These issues have to be carefully analysed and understood, so that sensible and helpful responses are made. The black community, and all working class communities, have to educate themselves and be responsible for preserving and defending their own culture. Social workers, if they are acting professionally, should respect people and treat them fairly and impartially, whatever their race or social background. A residential social worker (actually the Officer-in-Charge) once described how every Sunday the male partner of a black relationship would come around to beat up his girl friend. She never interfered, because 'it is part of their culture'. She did not seek to find out what the female partner thought, or whether she wanted help or whether she too saw the beatings as part of her cultural heritage.

These are the results of a lack of understanding and insight into human nature operating within a racist system which will tolerate ignorance as expertise – so long as it is black, and see beating up women as a natural part of black life. Child protection work must be about protecting children. In a multi-racial, plural society, where serial monogamy (divorce and remarriage) is a common part of many people's lives, it is not helpful to think in terms of a norm of family life – with black families providing some interesting ethnic diversion. Social work training must take account of this and equip social workers to work in a rapidly changing society, where the nature and composition of families does not remain static. Approached in this way it is possible to see black and other family styles as part of a range of ways of organising family life and rearing children.

Black social workers must identify the protection of children as their main concern and must work to improve the child protection service for all children. That is the only way of making sure that black children will receive as good or bad a service as any other child. The development of specialist black and ethnic monority units, whilst perhaps of short term value to black professionals, must in this context be seen as potentially detrimental to the interests of black children.

Some take the view that as black people we must 'keep these problems within the black/ethnic community', because both the welfare and criminal justice systems are racist. They argue that the disclosure of abuse within ethnic communities will be used to further stigmatize and marginalise these communities. Victims of abuse should not be expected to protect any community from the stigma of having abusers in its midst, all communities are blighted by such people. But the responsibility for any stigma belongs to the abuser and not to the victim. In relation to black and other ethnic communities – the system is no less racist for the victim than for the offender. In fact the victim will frequently have sexism to deal with as well as racism. These are complex and difficult problems, which require open and honest discussion, not knee-jerk reactions. Social workers should not collude with racism by denying black children the same rights to protection from abuse as any other child.

Summary of the Main Points
This chapter looked at contextual issues, focusing on these areas:

1) The organisation and structure of SSDs.

2) The inter-agency context, common problems and difficulties.

3) The law and the criminal justice system.

4) Social class – the selective nature of existing knowledge on class and child abuse, and the fact that this does not permit a view on the relationship between social class and child abuse, was acknowledged.

5) Gender – some of the implications of a predominantly female workforce under mainly male management were considered.

6) Race – illustrations were used to highlight the poverty of thought in this area, and the possibility of black and other ethnic minorities being less well protected than others, was identified and discussed.

Chapter 4

Coping with Child Protection Work
Focus on the Professional Dimension

This chapter is about surviving CPW by getting the best management, supervision and training, and by social workers making realistic demands of themselves. The areas selected for analysis, discussion and for further action are those which many practitioners have experienced as problematic. Social workers do not always impress the general public with their ability to identify and defend their own interests. But they do have legitimate interests, which are quite distinct from those of employers and clients. It is important to the quality of the service that practitioners are well served by the system which employs them. This book began with a reference to some of the problems social workers face in CPW and suggested that these can result in practitioners themselves becoming victims.

The contents of this chapter assume that social work professionals are prepared to identify and protect their interests. The term 'professional' is used in this context to define a group of people specially educated and trained to carry out a particular job of work which, without such education and training, they would not be competent to undertake. Job satisfaction and maintaining enthusiasm and commitment in any area of work is very important; it is especially important in the difficult and demanding area of CPW. In order to achieve any measure of job satisfaction in CPW social workers must make demands of the system. They must begin to develop survival skills, protecting themselves from unfair demands and pressures and from unsound training methods and techniques. They should refuse to accept personal responsibility for things over which they have no control – such as the effects of government policies. They must also be prepared to put time, energy and thought into understanding and influencing those areas over which they do have control.

When social workers are highly stressed, poorly trained and badly managed, it is hardly surprising that the service they give is less than good – and sometimes quite poor. Problems of practice may be reflective of factors other than the competence of practitioners. Practitioner competence is only one of many factors influencing outcome in CPW. Where a practitioner has problems, supportive and competent Management should be aware of weaknesses and should be targeting supervision, training, staff development and appraisal towards helping the worker to improve in these areas. It is in the interests of both the professional and also the public, whom they serve, that this basic support structure is available to the people who take on the difficult, complex and demanding tasks associated with CPW. We turn now to look at each of these areas in more detail.

Getting the Best out of Management and Supervision

The Local Government Training Board (1987) in a report on SSDs, commented that social services management is confused and unclear about its role and function. In an exercise which was undertaken as part of a research study into social work training for child protection work (Stone, 1988) a group of social services managers were asked to indicate the model of management which they felt was most appropriate in CPW. The models used were drawn from a DHSS publication (1986) and consists of three models of management, emphasising:

1) Compliance with rules.

2) Providing an objective viewpoint.

3) Providing emotional support and professional guidance to social workers.

The managers did not have a consistent view of the management role in CPW; they were as likely to see any one or all three models as of equal importance. The exceptions occurred in teams where there was an additional layer of professional child protection expertise between the manager and the social worker. This was provided by the 'Trainer Practitioners'. In teams where there were Trainer Practitioners, the managers were much clearer about their role and their views came closer to those of the social worker's (i.e. that the main management tasks in CPW are to ensure compliance with the law and procedures and to provide an objective viewpoint). This model allows a clear division between 'management' and 'professional' tasks. The Trainer Practitioners provide 'emotional support', without compromising the Management function of ensuring rule compliance and providing an objective viewpoint.

Social Services managers are not alone in being unclear about their role and function in relation to the purpose of the organisation. The problem is that they and their workers may not be all that happy about either the organisation or the work they have to do. In trying to resolve these problems the managers may interpret their management functions to make them more attractive and consistent with the managers' views and values. This might well mean identifying with the 'caring' part of the management role to the detriment of the more 'supervisory' parts of the work. To ensure that they get good management, social workers must have a clear idea of what for them is 'good management'. Do not confuse your managers by making inappropriate demands of them, look to them to fulfil their proper role and functions; they are not case workers to their staff. Do not encourage them to act as such. Make demands which are related to their role as managers, and encourage them to respond in these terms.

Social workers should use their communication skills to approach these matters in such a way that they are likely to receive a positive reaction. In case you find this difficult, try applying the following basic rules; be aware of how you frame an approach to management, does it put you in the role of 'client'? Is that what you want? Social work is a predominantly female profession, 74% of fieldworkers are female (ADSS, 1989 Workforce Survey), but they are mainly managed by males. It is easy for the female work force to replicate the dependency model in the work place and this fits in well with the client/professional model, which also reflects dependency and which is the traditional social work approach. There are factors which encourage both females and males in similar positions to accept, or even to prefer styles of management which may be detrimental to their interests.

Social workers sometimes develop peer-support networks where there is no specialist professional support available to them. Whilst in no way undervaluing peer support in itself, the nature of CPW suggests that this should be an optional extra, rather than the only means of professional support. Social workers should be very clear about the remit of peer-support groups, and the existence of such groups should not be used as an excuse for not providing proper professional support to practitioners.

Practitioner's CPW should be supervised by a person whose main or sole work is in the field of child protection and whose remit includes a 'developmental' as well as a supervisory function. This model of supervision answers the requirement for practitioners to receive emotional support, professional guidance and specialist expertise. It also frees the manager to 'manage', and assumes that this includes line management of the supervisor, with control over resource allocation etc.

Managers in SSDs are often placed in contradictory and conflicting roles in respect to child protection work. A line manager may be expected to provide on-going supervision of practitioner's work; to manage resource allocation and to decide on priorities between different types of work and different client groups. In CPW managers often take a direct role by chairing Case Conferences. Some of these roles are clearly incompatible; managers cannot provide an independent view on those cases in which they have been involved. In regard to overall priorities – social workers often feel themselves to be under pressure from Management to make CPW the absolute priority, irrespective of the needs of other clients. This reflects both the high profile of CPW and the active role which managers often have in these cases.

Practitioners should look to the CPW specialists for professional support and guidance in areas in which social work has been shown to fail or to be inadequate. They should then look for help with their own specific professional and personal developmental needs. In developing strategies to ensure adequate supervision, practitioners should begin by focusing on those areas which the DHSS Inspectors Report identified as problematic for the profession as a whole. They should then design, with their supervisors, their own framework for supervision and negotiate a contract which takes these on board.

Each supervision session should take one or more of these topics as its focal points; and this framework should also be used when presenting and discussing case material during supervision. Practitioners must come to supervision sessions ready and prepared to use them effectively; they must themselves input into the sessions by bringing information etc to the attention of supervisors. They must make demands of supervisors; this will feed into the supervisors own professional development and strengthen the service as a whole. In a sense, practitioners are being encouraged to take some responsibility for the supervision they receive and to become more actively involved in the whole process.

Hints for getting good/adequate Management and supervision in Child Protection Work

Making the most and getting the best out of Management:

1) Make sure that you understand the role and function of your Management in relation to CPW.

2) Make appropriate demands of Management in relation to their specific management brief.

3) Support Management in efforts to keep up to date with relevant training – managers also have their training needs.

4) Encourage managers to share information regarding agency problems, and the pressures they experience, as it were, from 'above'.

5) Feedback – always try to get feedback on how Management views your performance.

6) Use appraisal interviews etc as much for your benefit, as for the organisations.

7) Choose your timing well, especially when you are trying to raise difficult and sensitive issues.

8) Always keep a record of the main points of interviews and discussions.

9) Try to get agreements written or incorporated into some statement about intent.

Making the most and getting the best out of supervision:

1) It is essential to prepare for supervision sessions; begin by trying to link your child protection supervision sessions consciously to the four topics: recording; information gathering, identifying and coordinating relevant information; assessments – process, content, structure, aims and objectives; and supervision itself – its purpose, whether it is fulfilling its purpose? – check out expectations as against actuality.

2) Structure the time and the content of each session, come with your own agenda of items you wish to discuss.

3) Give your supervisor advanced notice of difficult or problematic areas you wish to discuss; if you have any relevant documentation, it would also be helpful to make copies available beforehand.

4) Use your case material to examine wider issues, and the implications of particular types of decision-making within the agency/organisation.

5) Be sure to relate your discussions to organisational and other problems when these are relevant, e.g. lack of resources, be specific in indicating the difference you think a resource input would make to each case.

6) Keep a written or taped record of your CPW supervision sessions; these will act as an aide memoire, and also assist in your personal and professional development.

7) Only bring in your personal life and background, especially in relation to any experience of abuse, if you judge these to be of relevance to your work.

8) Always seek a firm guarantee as regards confidentiality before disclosing private information about yourself.

9) You may wish to discuss the implications of such a disclosure with another, independent person before sharing it in a supervision session; your rights as a worker may well be compromised as a result of your actions in such matters.

10) Seek independent professional advice if you feel your personal life or your background may be affecting your CPW; this reduces the possibility of role confusion and stigmatisation.

A model of supervision which includes professional and developmental aspects, and offers practitioners the opportunity both to challenge and be challenged, is to be encouraged. Supervision in CPW must offer practitioners a supportive, but demanding experience, so that they can be extended and extend themselves in order to deliver the best child protection service.

Training

Training follows on naturally from the discussion of management and supervision. Training should be part of the package of on-going staff development and support in any system of good management. Unfortunately in the area of CPW, training has developed without any clear theoretical base, and with very little idea of the methods best suited to achieve training goals. CPW training has reflected many of the inherent tensions and problems in social work practice generally.

To move towards constructive suggestions for improving training in this field, it might be helpful to look at the reason why training is used in any work situation. The purpose of training is normally to produce changes in the attitudes, skills and knowledge of those exposed to the training. For the training to be deemed effective the changes must be more or less permanent. With training in physical tasks it is easy to demonstrate whether or not the trainee has acquired the skill component, but much less easy to demonstrate that attitudes towards the tasks have been affected by the training.

When training someone to be a car driver or to be a bricklayer, the trainer can test and the trainee can demonstrate whether the physical skills of car driving or bricklaying have been acquired. What is more difficult is to find our whether the trainee's attitudes to safety on the roads and on the building site have been affected by the process, content or method of training. Evidence suggests that in the examples discussed above a trainee's attitudes to safety are affected by training in the short term, but these gains are dissipated under the day-to-day pressures of car driving or bricklaying. There is a very real problem about sustaining training outcomes away from the immediate training context, with whatever the particular training effort is concerned.

If these observations are true about something like car driving or bricklaying, they must be even more true about professional training for CPW. In the above examples it is clear what the aims of the training are, at least in terms of its physical dimension, i.e. to drive a car; to be a bricklayer. But beyond that, problems emerge as to the degree of competence required to be a safe car driver or bricklayer. Going by the high casualty rate on the roads and on building sites, either the training is not effective for the conditions which people have to drive and work in, or it has no bearing on the casualty rates. In the context of work, training usually comes about in response to some identified need or demand from workers. In relation to CPW, increasing evidence from government inquiries, court cases etc, point to skill and knowledge deficits and problems with attitudes in the social work profession. In response to the criticisms which have been levelled at the profession, attempts have been made to develop and/or extend social work training for CPW.

Since, as has already been shown, the social work understanding of the definition, nature and extent of child abuse is partial and incomplete, the training efforts reflect this. The trainers are often not 'trained' in training, but are social workers who go into training departments and pick it up. They do not pick up the research into the effects of different training styles and methods; nor information on the advantages and disadvantages of different approaches. Thus training is undertaken as a social work exercise and has many of the values and approaches traditionally associated with casework. For example, if a course member questions something the question is likely to be seen, not as a valid part of a learning process but as an indication that the questioner is being 'defensive' and cannot 'deal with' the issue. This means that questions are either not posed or are filtered and put in a way that is thought will be acceptable. This does nothing to promote the training aims and goals of the exercises. The following example should help to illustrate the point being made. These comments are from Community Care 'Research' file (13 October, 1988) on problems on the use of anatomically correct dolls by social workers investigating allegations of sexual abuse. The author is reviewing an article which provides a set of guidelines on the use of the dolls. (It has to be assumed that the interviews are not with the dolls themselves, but with the children!). The writer states that:

> 'Many people using them are untrained, and those seeking training have found that little has been published on how to conduct or interpret investigative interviews with dolls. There is often lack of agreement on how to

present the dolls, structure the interview, and avoid leading the child.'

During a training course on sexual abuse, anatomical dolls were introduced and their use in the investigation and diagnosis of child sexual abuse was explained. Following this the dolls were handed around for the participants to examine. One of the male participants queried the necessity for handing the dolls around and encouraging close inspection of them. The response from the trainer was immediate, direct and quite clear – he had problems, sexual ones of course, that's the only explanation for his question. From a learning/ training viewpoint, the trainer's response was unhelpful. Why was it unhelpful to the learners? Because it stifled inquiry, it gave a message that only one view was acceptable and anyone questioning the 'gospel' was a heretic. That message may be alright for some religious leaders, but for a trainer? The example also shows the use of inappropriate models in social work training and the way the trainer's casework-type method was badly adapted to the training context.

As well as working against the training goals, some training methods pose difficult ethical problems. Research into the effects of different types of training methods show that training can have negative as well as positive outcomes. See Smith's (1975) analysis of the effects of sensitivity training; and Jaffe and Scherl (1969) for a discussion on psychosis precipitated by T-Group membership. Also Lakin (1969) for a discussion of the ethical issues involved in the use of so-called sensitivity training. Cooper and Bowles (1977) research suggests that exposure to these methods may be 'hurtful or helpful' to participants. Cooper and Bowles observed that although there are dangers and risks associated with these training methods, there are also some 'positive outcomes'. Positive outcomes are linked to groups with a high degree of structure, low levels of intimacy and little confrontation. Group members should be self-sufficient and somewhat controlled and the trainers should be supportive, relaxed and with low anxiety levels. Cooper and Bowles also suggest screening to exclude vulnerable people.

There is no evidence to suggest that these observations do not apply equally to social workers as to managers in industry (the training groups which Cooper and Bowles studied). Social work trainers justify their use of confrontation and emotions on the grounds that if 'people can't cope with the techniques they shouldn't be in social work'. This shows that they are confused about their role as trainers; trainers are not supposed to be deciding who is suitable for a job or profession, they are meant to be helping those already in the job to do it better.

Much of the child protection training currently available to social workers uses questionable methods. These methods have not been assessed for their effect on individuals, or for their efficacy in achieving training goals. These methods make use of pictures, videos and slides which are very explicit in their portrayal of abused children. What is the effect of constant exposure to such stimuli? Does using this material actually contribute towards the learning outcome, or conversely, inhibit learners' acquisition of skills and knowledge? There is also the danger that people may become desensitized as a result of exposure to human distress and suffering, presented in an artificial, almost technical way. See Horncastle and Bull (1985) for a discussion of some unintended consequences of training, and Yalom and Lieberman's (1971) study of 'casualties' of group training.

Learning theory and knowledge of the conditions which promote adult learning, suggest that an emotional atmosphere is not conducive to learning. People in a condition of heightened feelings, are not generally well placed to acquire new knowledge, or to retain anything they have learnt. It is therefore bad practice in educational terms, and against the aims of the whole exercise, for trainers to allow such atmospheres to develop. Many courses have allowed people to be crying and to be in varying states of distress, not only are participants on such courses distressed at the time, but many also often suffer trauma later on as a direct result of attending training courses. (See Celia Doyle's article *Management Sensitivity – An Issue in Child Sexual Abuse Training*, 1986.)

Are social work trainer's involved in therapy or training? Sometimes its hard to tell the difference. But the difference should be obvious; in therapy a person enters a relationship with another person to seek a particular kind of help, the therapist has a professional duty towards the client and the encounter takes place within that context. In work-related training, people who are doing a job of work expose themselves to training which they hope will improve their competence.

Many have argued, and will argue, that the methods used are intended to provoke and unleash feelings; that unless social workers are able to go through this process and to deal with such feelings, particularly in relation to sexual abuse, they will not be able to work effectively in this field. Where is the evidence for this claim? Does it apply with equal force to all areas of social work practice? Where are the sanctions against those who show themselves unable or unwilling to respond to such methods? There are none. There is no evidence that these training methods work or that they are necessary; indeed, what evidence there is causes one to wonder about the potential damage they may cause. Damage may occur in two ways;

directly to the individuals undergoing the training and indirectly by triggering feelings and responses in people they were not aware they had and changing their behaviour in a negative way. For example, triggering violent or aggressive tendencies in people or encouraging sexual fantasies, which led them to act in an uncharacteristic way. Whilst knowledge about the causes of abuse remains so inadequate, training has a particular responsibility not to encourage, in any way, conditions which may give rise to abuse.

There is another aspect of training for CPW which should be considered; in such training exercises, participants are often encouraged, either explicitly or implicitly, to talk about their own experience of abuse. The same point, as regards the remit of training and the remit of therapy, has to be made. In therapy the feelings which are released as a result of such disclosures must be addressed by the therapist, and adequate support given to help the client manage any resulting crisis. In training there are no such safeguards; and participants are not informed about the risks associated with particular training methods nor given the choice as to whether or not they want to take part.

Social Work Trainers are not generally professionally qualified in training, but have been recruited direct from social work practice. Their approach to training often seems to have more in common with providing therapy than with teaching and learning. It also means that these trainers are often unaware of the risks associated with particular training methods and of the relevant research. For example, there is no screening out of vulnerable people and usually no support to help such people cope with any negative effects of the training. Keisler's (1973) study of emotions in group training, suggests that triggering feelings in this way is likely to be detrimental to some participants. Trainers have a duty to inform participants if the methods they intend using will involve the disclosure of personal information or cause distress in any way; to explain the reasons for the use of particular training methods and techniques in terms of the achievement of training outcomes; to identify safeguards and support for those at risk. Such support should be independent of the participants' employing agency. Social workers must have the confidence to challenge trainers about the methods and techniques they employ; and organisations must ensure that trainers are accountable and accept responsibility for training outcomes.

The content of training for CPW must also address social issues such as gender, race and class, in terms of their impact on the values and attitudes of practitioners. These issues also affect decision making in relation to the allocation of cases, so there are practical reasons for training to take these on board in an explicit way. There has to be much discussion, consultation and research on the best way to go about this; but there is currently no information available which would facilitate developments along the lines suggested. However, there is evidence (Stone, 1988) of tensions between the trainers interest in 'feelings' as the focus of training and practitioners interest in acquiring skills. The trainers approach reflects their own professional background as social workers and the lack of an identifiable 'training' as opposed to 'social work' philosophy to underpin their work. Practitioners face difficult and sometimes dangerous situations in CPW; it is understandable that they want training to be skills related.

The transfer of training – how learners apply the skills and knowledge they have acquired in the training context, to the road, the building site or the next child protection referral – is of critical importance to this discussion. One possible solution is to move to a work-based training approach. Work-based training removes a lot of the problems we have been discussing, relevance is obvious as the training relates to the work in which people are currently involved. Trainers need to be properly trained themselves and materials must be developed or adapted; it is a challenge, but it can be done. As managers and practitioners consider the advantages of work-based training, hopefully it will become more common. In the meantime social workers should reflect on their experiences of training for CPW, and examine the main impact such training has had on them as professionals and as people. In trying to influence the direction and quality of future training in their agencies, they must ask some of the fundamental questions about the purpose, method and accountability of trainers.

Before leaving this section, a word about training for inter-agency work. It is obvious that social work has quite a lot to do in clearing up its own training agenda, CPW takes place within an inter-agency context and appropriate training is required. Child protection agencies should develop proper training policies, with training in skills relevant to inter-agency work an integral part of the training for CPW. This requires a systematic assessment of training needs, based on an analysis of the skills, knowledge and attitudes which are required in the inter-agency context. This provides a sound basis for the development of good inter-agency training for practitioners.

Hints for getting good training

1) Encourage your Management to define its training policy, don't be put off by waffle.

2) Find out what methods, if any, the organisation uses to monitor and evaluate training.

3) Get examples of other similar agencies and organisations training policies to show what you mean by a 'training policy'.

71

4) Get your department to develop proper policies – re training; CPW etc – note that SSDs will often put forward statements of principles as 'policies' – do not be taken in by these.

5) Encourage your Team to discuss and consult together on training needs and about the efficacy of different training methods and techniques.

6) When you feedback to your Team or management on a training experience use a structured framework, and be specific about what the course covered, the methods used, and how you intend to apply what you've learnt in your CPW.

7) Encourage colleagues to do the same; this will enable your organisation to make informed choices when commissioning future training from outside trainers/agencies.

8) In-house training should reflect a discussion and consultation process – encourage this through feedback.

9) Be confident in challenging Trainers over their methods if you have cause for concern; ask about feedback from previous course participants/agencies; and whether the Trainer is aware of any research/evaluation on the methods being used.

10) Encourage the development or at least the discussion of more work-based training for child protection work.

The Theory Deficit

It has been suggested that the social work theory deficit has serious implications for CPW. In which areas is this deficit most apparent, and what are these implications? Three areas which illustrate these problems very well are:

1) The tensions between 'casework' and community social work.

2) The definition of child abuse as exclusively or mainly a 'family problem'.

3) Social issues of gender, race and class as these relate to and impact on professional social work practice and CPW.

(1) *Casework and community social work – Barclay revisited*

Chapter 1 presented a brief outline of the factors which influenced the development of the social work profession. It was suggested that, although social work practice developed among poor people and mainly in response to social and economic problems, the theory on which it was based did not reflect these origins. Hence the growth of community social work in response to the inadequacies and deficits of traditional approaches which explained social problems in terms of individual and family pathology. In contrast, community social work encouraged a more participative, less stigmatising approach, with a focus on the group/community/neighbourhood. Unfortunately community social work emerged at a time when the profession was experiencing rapid change – in particular development of SSDs. This coincided with or resulted in an expansion in the statutory role of social work, which does not fit well with a community social work approach.

In 1982, the then Secretary of State for Social Services, established a committee of inquiry to examine and report on 'the roles and tasks' of social workers. This Committee was chaired by Peter Barclay; the report took its name from the chair and came to be known as The Barclay Report (1982). The terms of reference of the Committee were: 'to review the role and tasks of social workers in local authority Social Services Departments and related voluntary agencies in England and Wales and to make recommendations'. The Committee was the result of massive criticism of social work, in which the need for the profession was questioned – 'Do we need social workers?'. In its concluding paragraph the answer was given in the affirmative:

> 'In spite of all the complexities and uncertainties surrounding the functions of social workers, we are united in our belief that the work they do is of vital importance in our society . . . It is here to stay, and social workers are needed as never before.'

The Barclay Report was seen by many as a vindication of the social work profession; social work had been put on trial and, although not perfect, had emerged from the process with an endorsement and confirmation that the work it undertakes is essential to society. But there was a fly in the ointment, and this was Professor Pinker's minority report. Whilst it did not differ from the majority report in terms of its vindication of social work, it did take a very different view on the methods which social workers should employ in carrying out their role and function. To inform those not familiar with the arguments, and to remind those who are, briefly the debate centered on 'community social work' and the viability of method and practices based on this approach in relation to their statutory work in local authority SSDs. In essence Professor Pinker in his Minority Report argued that the statutory work which social workers were called upon to perform in SSDs and related voluntary agencies, ruled out community social work as an appropriate response.

In his 'alternative' proposal Professor Pinker argued that community social work was too woolly a concept, and that its use would undermine social work practice. To quote Pinker's words:

> 'The efficient and humane discharge of social work duties calls for specialised legal, psychological and social knowledge. Apart from practice skills, social workers must have a clear and detailed knowledge of the aspects of the law which affect their dealings with child protection, care and supervision . . . . . . In practice a great deal of social work is a task of "maintenance", control and support . . . .'

Following this analysis Professor Pinker argued for a specialised social work model (which acknowledged the true nature of the social work task) rather than a 'community social work' model which he saw as muddled and confused. This model he claimed inherently denied the true nature of the social work task in the SSDs, and Professor Pinker challenged the notion of 'community' and dismissed the concept as an illusion. Professor Pinker argued that the values and philosophy of community social work are at odds with the work which social workers actually have to carry out. Events since 1982 have proved Pinker to have been more or less right, at least in relation to CPW.

SSDs are operating more and more as a statutory service, with children's services as the dominant activity. This is closer to the Pinker model of a specialist service than to the general welfare model favoured by the rest of the Committee. The tensions between the value base of community social work and the policing, investigative and controlling role of statutory child protection work were well anticipated by Pinker. These tensions increase the problems and difficulties which social workers experience; they cannot look to their professional training for a body of knowledge which helps them to understand how to respond to the complexities of the issues they face. Traditional approaches are deficient but more recent developments still do not meet these shortcomings.

Practitioners complain that they are trained in community social work methods which stress partnership with, and accountability to, the community. But in practice they find that they have to police such communities, keeping records and notes of suspicious goings on and, if necessary, act against members of that community. Many practitioners feel very uncomfortable about the ethics of what they are doing and again Pinker pointed out the potential conflicts and contradictions in these roles. This suggests that at some point in time the purely welfare service provision role of SSDs will have to separate from the statutory, controlling and policing role. One benefit of this is that it will enable people entering the profession to make sensible choices about where they want to work; and the kind of work they want to do.

In the meantime people have to work within existing structures, but an understanding of the underlying issues and the context within which things developed to be as they are, may be helpful. To reduce the possibility of misunderstandings arising in areas where 'Patch' based community social work is the model of practice, information should be provided to the community in the form of leaflets, posters etc and with examples showing how social workers actually carry out their duties and discharge their responsibilities. The community has to be educated to accept things as they are and to work with the SSDs to protect children. At the same time, there is the right to privacy of members of the community and the duty of social workers not to mislead or misinform the community about their role and function in that community or neighbourhood.

(2) *Definition of child abuse as a predominantly 'family problem'*

Confused and muddled thinking is illustrated in the social work definition of sexual abuse. In the social work literature the term incest is often used interchangeably with the term child sexual abuse. The implication being that they are virtually the same thing. Conferences and training events which give as their theme 'child sexual abuse' in fact almost always deal with incest, or sexual abuse within the family. Training also reflects this conceptual problem and further reinforces a limited and partial view of child abuse. With increasing evidence showing the widespread and pervasive nature of child sexual abuse; with allegations (*The Independent* op cit) that sexual abuse may be happening in 75% of boarding schools – the social work definition imposes severe limitations on practitioners.

The following anecdote, drawn from many such will help to illustrate some of these points. A young female student whilst on placement in a Children's Home, complained to her visiting Tutor about unsuitable videos which the children were allowed to watch. She was advised by her (male) tutor that she was not placed there to spy on the staff; and no further information was sought or given. Towards the end of her training and during the course of another fieldwork visit, she explained to her new (female) tutor that in spite of passing both placements and the course she was thinking of not pursuing a career in social work. In the course of a long discussion she revealed what had occurred early on in her training, the nature of the 'unsuitable videos' (explicit blue movies) and the fact that many of the children and young people in the Children's Home had been placed there because of abuse.

In a state of some distress, she described some of the things which she had observed during her residential placement, she suspected that sexual activities had occurred between staff and children

75

following the films – but she had no proof of this. She talked of her abortive attempts to get something done and how this placed her own career in jeopardy. She felt that she had let the children down and blamed herself for not protecting them. This is not an isolated case, but it is a useful illustration of the way such matters are dealt with. If the student had reported that a parent was known to be showing pornographic videos to their children, the response would have been immediate. But in residential child care, children who are in care because of abuse could not be protected from further abuse; a system to ensure protection for children in these circumstances does not exist.

The value base of social work is essentially optimistic, based on a belief in the essential goodness of people, and that all human beings have the capacity for change and growth. Social workers think that they can help to provide these conditions for people whose experience of life has damaged them. Whilst these humanistic or even religious values are laudable, it is difficult to see how they address such matters as the sexual exploitation of children on a commercial scale. Or, as has been alleged in the Kincora Boy's Home scandal, the use of children in residential care to supply sex on an organised scale.

The tendency has been to fit new social problems into existing theoretical frames; in social work the existing frame is 'the family' so that framework both determines the location of, and the response to, new social problems. There is a pressing need for social work to identify and define child abuse and exploitation in terms other than 'the family'. Until this happens it will not be possible to offer children anything like a comprehensive child protection service. Practitioners should be in the forefront of the development of such a theory, but the conditions must be created which will make this possible. In the meantime practitioners should begin the process of getting to grips with the fundamental issues which are at the heart of the debate about theory and practice in CPW.

(3) *Social issues: class, gender and race*

Child protection work takes place in a society which is class based and in which women and racial monorities are generally disadvantaged. It is inevitable that social work will reflect these structural inequalities. Social work theory does not provide the tools to analyse and understand these issues and problems as the basis for developing good practice. It is not enough to rely on a sociological analysis of social class. Social work has to go beyond that and begin to develop an identifiable social work perspective on these issues.

The British Association of Social Work called for a 'black perspective' in social work. This has been interpreted in different ways by various people and agencies, sometimes, it seems, adding to the difficulties and problems already facing black people in Britain. The inherent problems of confused and muddled thinking are reflected in this area to the detriment of the quality of service offered to black children. Social workers have to have confidence in their professional skills and judgments, and be guided by the necessity to protect children. They must not let fears of being branded racist or whatever, deter them from carrying out their work. There is a job for black social workers and those from other minority groups to educate and inform our communities about the child care remit of the statutory social services, and to encourage the strengths of such communities in their concern, interest in and protection of children. However, once the need arises for the State to intervene, it must offer the same quality of service and the same safeguards to all citizens.

Children from minority communities will be protected only so far as all children are protected; if the service is basically poorly resourced and staff are badly trained and badly supported in their work, that will effect the services, whatever the colour and race of the worker. This does not mean that social work educators and trainers should ignore the task of preparing and training professionals for a racially mixed and culturally diverse society. Training methods and the teaching curriculum must reflect these needs. It is also taken as read that the staffing and management profile of social work agencies will reflect the composition of the communities they serve.

Those who look to the recruitment of black social workers to produce major changes in social work service delivery and quality to black clients, would do well to reflect on the fact that women clients have not gained very much from a social work service staffed mainly by women. The reverse has probably been more true, with some female social workers adopting harsh, blaming and condemnatory attitudes towards women clients. The definition of child abuse as a 'family problem' unfairly targets women, and is the basis of the colluding-mother stereotype. This is the result of existing ideas and perceptions being grafted on to meet new challenges. The result has been an uncomfortable fit, with big gaps, which contributes to the demoralization and uncertainty of workers.

A social work theory of CPW would also confront the question of values in a coherent and rational way. The process of analysing and defining the extent and nature of child abuse in terms other than family malfunction must begin. The next logical step would be to develop some theory on which to base an intervention strategy. The process would involve coming to some assessment of how far existing social work values could form the basis for new and different methods of intervention. It may be that social work values as presently understood do not sustain practitioners in some areas of

CPW. It may be that these actually add to the problems, in that practitioners are put in a double bind, by acting in ways which they consider are contrary to their professional values. Social workers often feel very angry, hateful and punitive towards offenders, especially in some of the more gross examples of sexual abuse and child rape which they have to deal with. Their professional values and training tells them to be non-judgmental and caring towards people whatever they have done. Some practitioners find this impossible to do, and equally impossible to admit to not doing. So they live and work in a state of what is known as 'cognitive dissonance', where there is a discrepancy between belief and action. The usual result is nearly always an increase in personal stress brought on as a result of being in a state of conflict.

Specialist Child Protection Units – the pros and cons

Specialist Child Protection Units (CPU) have been developed mainly as a defensive reaction to media and public opinion. Very little attempt at a systematic process of investigation and analysis has been undertaken with regard to: (a) whether specialist units are necessary, (b) how they should be staffed, (c) how their work would fit in and relate to other activities and (d) how staff would be trained and supported. The role and function of specialist units in all types of service delivery requires clear justification, in relation to the possible duplication of services and the optimum length of time staff should be attached to such units, bearing in mind the specialist nature of the work.

Child sexual abuse as a specialist area of CPW is a particularly worrying development of specialist units. There is no obvious reason why sexual abuse should not be dealt with professionally with a general child protection service. The reason why sexual abuse has received this mantle is unclear and requires further examination. It is unlikely that such Units would provide professionals with a range of work experiences on which to base their professional development. This in turn has implications for the way professionals approach specialist work. Exposure to a variety of methods, clients groups and communities is likely to result in an altogether different type of professional than one who has worked exclusively in a particular field. The nature of CPW would suggest that the service is best provided within mainstream service provision. Practitioners will benefit from retaining a balanced work load, and children will benefit from professionals who are not exhausted and drained of imagination and ideas, as a result of constant exposure to child misery. Practitioners have to ask themselves serious questions about how they themselves are likely to fare as persons and as professionals with an unvaried and concentrated case load of this kind.

Public Opinion and Media Phobia – the Impact on Child Protection Work

Child protection has a very high media profile and social workers and their managers operate on a day-to-day basis to cover themselves in case they are the next in line for media attention. The media exerts a very strong influence on service provision and decision making in CPW. Media influence is ever present and pervasive; social workers, when asked about the way they make decisions or respond to competing demands from clients, invariably respond that CPW takes precedence over all other types of work. This is partly as a result of departmental policy, but mainly because they fear 'being the next social worker to make front page news'. Clearly this is a distorting effect, the impact of which we can only guess. It is more than likely that media phobia played some part in the events in Cleveland, at least in terms of the SSD's response, although this was never identified as a contributing factor. However, knowledge and experience of the effect of the media suggests that social workers and their managers 'over-react' in a bid to protect themselves from attracting media attention.

It is completely unacceptable that the media, and very often this means the gutter press, should dictate the social work response to child protection problems. In the National Health Service, patients not infrequently die or are injured because of medical negligence or as a result of mistakes, but the media does not dictate how doctors carry out their day-to-day work. Other professionals also unfortunately perform badly from time to time, but none come in for the treatment meted out to social workers who fail. Social workers must be accountable and the media has a legitimate interest in keeping the public informed, but the influence of the media seem to go well beyond this. It may well be that this subject requires further investigation to detail exactly how and to what extent the media is controlling the social worker's response to child protection. But practitioners should also make a conscious effort to reduce the influence which the media exerts on their decision making. Legal and professional considerations should be the guiding factors – not media phobia. There are dangers of too great a reaction to public opinion producing a distorting effect on provision. It is essential that this does not happen in CPW.

The high media attention which child protection issues attract, may also have other effects, some positive, others less so. Amongst the positive is the greater awareness of child abuse and hopefully a willingness for responsible citizens to assist in protecting children. On the negative side is the tolerance which may result as more and more revelations are made, and as the public grow used to such occurrences. There is also the possibility that such revelations act as a magnet attracting people with questionable motives into residential and field social work. These are aspects which are not often considered, but should be, since they clearly have important implications for the profession.

Summary of the Main Points
This chapter considered some of the professional problems and issues which affect the quality of CPW, including:

1) Management and supervision – with tips and hints on how to get the best from and make the most of the existing system;

2) Training came next with an examination of the aims, objectives, content and methods of training for CPW.

3) This chapter returned to social work theory, looking in particular at the role of community social work.

4) The social issues of class, race and gender were discussed from the perspective of the individual worker.

5) The question of the role of specialist child protection units, and the implications of such units for practitioner's and for the child protection service was considered.

6) The influence of public opinion and the media were discussed in relation to their impact on CPW. The influence of the media was considered to be quite disproportionate in affecting practitioners response.

Chapter 5

Child Protection Work – the Personal Dimension

This chapter focuses on child protection workers as people with the normal human weaknesses. We look at the way CPW affects people as parents, husbands, wives, partners – friends of victims. Child protection workers are themselves members of different social groups whether defined by class, race or gender. They may also be perpetrators. Their work is undoubtedly highly stressed; what is the effect of such stress on individuals and how can they manage it so that they continue to function adequately, and achieve some measure of job satisfaction?: These matters are the subject of this chapter.

Child Protection Work – Professionals as Parents
'Those with children find it particularly difficult . . . . they think of their own children.'
(Team Manager, male, no children).

'The worst case I had, it gave me nightmares, was of a little girl of three . . . . my own daughter was also just three at the time, I would look at her and see that child . . . . it was a long time before it passed.'
(Social Worker, mother).

All jobs have difficulties and problems, challenges and disappointments. CPW, by its very nature and by its history, is probably unique in its exclusive concern with preventing or responding to violence and the sexual exploitation of children. As the scale of abuse becomes known and SSDs and allied agencies expand their response, social workers find themselves and their personal and professional value systems tested and challenged every day. As parents themselves, they react just like any 'ordinary' parent: as professionals, they are expected to put such reactions and feelings aside. Yet support and help is not available to assist them in this process, and the professional values which they inherited from their professional training may create additional tensions, rather than helping to resolve any of them.

Apart from such moral and ethical problems, there are other ways in which social work professionals have been affected in their personal roles as parents, these include:

1) Threats of violence to their children.

2) Threats to kidnap the CP worker's children.

3) CP worker's deep fears and worries for the safety of their children.

4) High anxiety levels about the risks their children may face e.g. from paedophiles – 'You begin to think everyone is a paedophile.'

5) Reasonable and unreasonable fears that one of the spin-offs of the work they are doing may be to draw them into abusive behaviour; or conversely into being over anxious and over-protective parents.

Professional CPW is very likely to heighten normal parental anxieties, and there is a very real danger of such parents over-reacting and becoming over-protective. The high public and media profile which CPW attracts also contributes to pressures on the workers' families, and their children can be targeted for unpleasant attention. It is very difficult to think of any parallels in other occupations or professions, or even in the main body of social work itself. It is therefore understandable that people feel isolated and unsupported in this aspect of their lives and find it difficult to talk about these problems. Professionals are placed in a very difficult situation, where as parents they may have legitimate worries and anxieties, but as 'experts' themselves they are expected, and expect themselves, to cope with all eventualities. There is virtually no opportunity to acknowledge and learn to manage the occupational hazards of the work. There is often no acknowledgment of these aspects of the work, and little attempt to address such issues in training.

Child protection agencies should consider providing independent counselling and support for social workers who, as parents, experience a high degree of stress and anxiety in connection with this work. Child protection professionals should press for employers to provide this service in acknowledgement of the hazards and dangers associated with CPW. Some employing organisations take the view that since only experienced (i.e. Level Three workers) are employed in CPW, they should be able to cope with all the demands of the job. This denies the reality that all workers are not experienced; and that many lack adequate training, which makes it virtually impossible for them to make demands of the system without appearing to be 'inadequate' themselves.

Mothers and fathers experience things differently and they react differently to the same pressures. The area of sexual abuse is of particular interest in this regard. Some people report a loss of interest in sex as a result of their work, whilst some experience the opposite effect and are 'turned on' by some of the things to which they are exposed. Male workers also become very conscious of the dangers of becoming abusers by virtue of, say, being a stepfather. Several male social workers and managers have expressed these concerns during research interviews. One male social worker put it this way:

> 'It is very difficult when you see men, just like yourself in other respects . . . . not to consider the possibility that you might act in this way . . . . I feel this as a stepfather of an adolescent teenage girl. I am very conscious of the dangers there . . . . my work has made me conscious, and I do a lot to avoid problems or misunderstandings . . . . how much this is necessary, I don't know . . . . but its the way I've taken to dealing with the situation because of what I've seen in my work where this type of abuse has occurred . . . .'

A proper analysis of the work and of its associated risks and dangers would enable a rational response. People cannot split themselves into disparate entities, and undoubtedly performance is affected by workers experiences as parents, and the other way round. If agencies are interested in improving work performance, they must look to the issues which impact on and influence the individuals ability to function adequately. Professionals may find it useful to examine their situation as parents using objective, rational criteria to assess the risks to their children, and as the basis for strategies to reduce, offset or cancel out such risks. They should also encourage their professional organisations to press for independent counselling/advice to be available on request to those who judge that such assistance would be helpful to them. This point will be reinforced time and time again in this chapter as we continue to examine and reflect on the personal dimension in CPW.

Professionals as Survivors of Child Abuse

The best way into this subject may well be by way of a story; this story raises many of the problems and difficulties around this area. This story is given by way of a morality tale, of good intentions gone wrong and the way individuals, agencies and ultimately consumers suffer as a result.

A newly established Child Protection Team worked with a philosophy of encouraging the workers who had had such experiences to be explicit about them, and to use these experiences in their work with clients. This worked well to begin with, but as things developed and as tensions manifested themselves at all levels of the organisation, the survivors were increasingly used as scapegoats. They were accused of over-identifying with the clients, of not being 'objective' and, of undermining the approach of the agency. As with most situations of this type, the matter was resolved through staff turnover, as people – mainly the survivors – left for other jobs.

No one at the time identified the problems in terms of survivors being scapegoated and ultimately driven out. It was mainly as a result of the tensions re-surfacing subsequently, and with the help of an independent outsider, that the history of the team was untangled. It became clear that the team had started out with a view of survivors as professionals, which was based on the belief that such experiences provided useful insights, which the survivors would bring to their work. The survivors accepted this and were therefore open and honest about their experiences of abuse. They felt safe within a specialist group, with a philosophy which seemed to value their experiences and was prepared to use them. However, under pressure of the work, understaffed and facing the usual problems of lack of adequate support etc, this broke down, and the values and philosophy of the team came under pressure. Many of the problems troubling the team were put at the door of team members who had defined themselves as survivors of various kinds of child abuse.

An analysis of what went on in this team, and the suffering which was caused to individuals shows the team's approach to be extremely naive and simplistic. The team ignored the right of the staff members to privacy in asking and encouraging people to be 'open' about any past abuse. No assurances were asked for, or given, about what would be done with this information. There was an assumption that everyone involved would be able to act with proper regard to the interest of the individual and the team. No provision was made for persons affected by the appeal for openness, to have any support or counselling to help them cope with any consequences. Nor were the organisational issues identified in terms of agency goals and the needs and interests of clients. There was just a general assumption that such disclosures by staff members would promote the goals of the agency's child protection work. This lack of awareness and the limitations in the perception of those involved meant that most of the staff members who had been victims of abuse, resigned.

There must be other more successful attempts to use the experiences of professionals who are survivors of abuse. But the idea itself remains suspect, both in terms of its underlying assumptions and of its practical outcomes. The underlying assumptions that the individual would be respected, proved wrong. As did the assumption that it was beneficial to the team and the agency to adopt this approach in the first place. Under the pressures of the work, people fell back on stereotype behaviour and attitudes, explaining differences not in terms of different professional approaches, but in terms of the personal life history of those who held opposing points of view. So that particular approaches were defined, not in terms of their value to the users, but to the people with whom they were associated. This process marginalised those who were survivors, who went on the defensive and attacked their colleagues for being reactionary, or whatever. It is not hard to imagine the tension in the team as they tried to sort out these problems and the way the work suffered as a result.

It should be obvious that child protection work has been viewed throughout this book as a highly skilled, very demanding job. Workers in this field should not expose themselves to additional pressures by giving way to encouragement to 'share' their experiences of abuse. It is necessary to ask some very basic questions about what such 'sharing' involves, and how workers' rights to personal privacy will be safeguarded. Such questions include how the information will be used, who will have access to it, and what safeguards exist to ensure that it will not become, for example, part of a personnel file? Even then there are unintended consequences for the individual and the organisation, which cannot be anticipated, as was shown in the above example. If there were Health and Safety rules specially designed for CPW this is the kind of area on which such rules would have to focus. A social worker's psychological and emotional health may well be put at risk by assumptions which, when subjected to critical analysis, have very little to recommend them.

Professionals who have survived child abuse have enough to cope with without being case material for agency practice. There is no justification in theory or practice for using people in this way and workers should resist such attempts where possible. If not, they should at least seek assurances about the confidentiality of the information and ensure that it is only used for an agreed purpose – say in supervision.

Caution is the word in all these matters, there is a clear need to think through some of the issues and not to simply react on the basis that disclosure is inherently a good thing. In the context of the work situation, the guiding principle, both for the individual worker and the agency, must be the promotion of agency goals. The managers and supervisors are not therapists and the workers are not there for purposes of therapy. At the same time, the need for therapy may arise in this or other types of work, and such help should be available to those who need it, but must be offered independently of the workplace.

Coping with 'Disclosures' in Social Situations

Inevitably, when friends and relatives know that a person is a child care professional involved with CPW, occasions arise when the history of past abuse is disclosed. Such disclosures may come from friends, relatives, spouses, partners, or from the person's own grown-up children – for instance revealing that they were 'touched up' or worse by baby sitters, scoutmasters etc.

Very often the last thing the professional wants is to have to confront and deal with these problems in their own private lives. Away from work, most people want to live 'normal' lives, but sometimes this is not possible. Take, for example, the situation of a newly married man, he is currently undergoing a course in connection with his work, no problem there. Except that he is a social worker and the course in question is on child protection. Naturally his wife is interested in his work and they talk about the course generally, again no problem, until the course and their conversation touches on the sexual abuse of children. The atmosphere becomes difficult and the husband gets the impression that his wife does not want to know about that aspect of his work. He pursues this, and eventually discovers that his wife had been sexually abused as a child. This information has a devastating effect on him; he feels 'completely shattered' by it and is unable to turn to anyone for help in sorting out his feelings.

He feels that such reactions, whilst understandable in any other man, are not acceptable in him, who as a professional, should have the advantage over ordinary people in such matters. He also finds that his attitude towards his wife is affected, likewise with his in-laws.

The disclosure has set off a train of feelings and events over which he seems to have very little control. Would it have been better not to have pressed the matter with his wife in the first place? It is for everyone to make their own judgments and, if faced with the same situation, ultimately their own decision. But awareness of the likelihood of such happenings and of their consequences might hopefully prepare people for such eventualities. In the case of the young man discussed above, the problems sorted themselves out over time, and he and his wife learnt to live with what had happened. They decided against involving other people, and coped as best they could.

Everyone reading this story will be reminded of their own experiences; and of how they coped or failed to cope with such experiences. It is important to note once again that not everyone is affected in the same way, or has the same reactions to similar experiences. Others may have more realistic ideas about themselves and do not expect to be perfect in these or similar circumstances.

Professionals as Perpetrators

On 24 June 1989, *The Guardian* ran the following news item. Under the headline *Children's Home Inquiry Demand*, it reported that Ms Clare Short, Labour MP for Birmingham Ladywood, had called for an independent inquiry into Birmingham's child care services by the Social Inspectorate. This demand was in response to suicide attempts by three children living at Acorn Grove Children's Home. Where, as the report stated:

'Last year five staff received payoffs totalling £18,000 after the authority decided not to go ahead with disciplinary proceedings because of the cost. They had been suspended after children at the home alleged that they had been hit with snooker cues, handcuffed to radiators and beaten. The staff denied the allegations.'

Another press report which is of interest comes from *Community Care*, 23 February 1989, again a news report, under the headline *Ryall's Pension Allowed* , it reported that:

'Payment to be made to Calderdale's former social services director Rod Ryall amounts to his share of government superannuation scheme . . . Calderdale's personnel sub-committee had decided against approaching the Secretary of State because the offenses took place in Ryall's own time and in his own home. He (Ryall) is serving a six-year prison sentence after being convicted of seven sexual offenses against teenage boys.'

And again from *Community Care* on 27 April, 1989 under the headline *Calls for Suspension of Greenwich Director*, the following news reported:

'Greenwich director Martin Manby was this week fielding calls for his suspension after an independent inquiry was launched into allegations of sexual abuse and sexual harassment at a secure unit for girls . . . Fay (Councillor Fay) wrote to the health minister David Mellor . . . He listed a number of alleged abuses by staff including sexual abuse, sexual harassment, strip searching and violence towards residents.'

This is a very difficult area to write about; not only does it accept that professionals can also be offenders, but in doing so, it directly challenges myths about child abuse in terms of its origins and location. But difficult though it is, it has to be done not least in order to assist in the goal of child protection, but also to help individuals identify potentially dangerous situations to which they may be exposed, and to take action to avoid such situations arising where possible. It has already been noted that the high media profile which child abuse cases attract may well be a factor in a certain type of person being drawn into the profession. Social work is no different from other professions in that respect, such risks are there, and the selection and recruitment process into the profession must take them into account. A further risk, when people are already part of the profession, is exposure to information or material which may trigger a side of them which otherwise would remain latent. Reference has already been made to this with respect to the use of certain techniques and materials.

Since so little is known about the factors which predispose towards abuse, people are not aware of what to look for in themselves and others. This is another way in which the exclusive focus on 'the family' has done a disservice to children. It is very rare to see, in any books or articles written on the subject of child abuse, any attempt to identify and analyse the non-family dimension. In the last year in Britain there have been reports of staff in Children's Homes being suspended and subsequently paid off for physically abusing children, (Birmingham, above); of staff being sent to prison for sexually abusing children in a Children's Home in Kent; and of calls for the resignation of the Director of Social Services in Greenwich where sexual abuse and exploitation of children in care is alleged to have occurred.

Undoubtedly there is physical and sexual abuse and emotional neglect in non-family settings. It is simply untrue to claim such behaviour requires a complex family situation in order for abuse to occur. Anyone who has the care of and responsibility for children can be offenders, and that includes child care professionals. Such abuse may result from the arbitrary exercise of the professional's power over the child (another definition of emotional abuse?) or by the professional physically or sexually abusing the child or young person. Although by its very nature the residential context offers the maximum opportunity for most types of abuse, abuse can occur in any context.

Sexual abuse by field social workers is not unknown; indeed a male field social worker explained his rationale for having sex with as many of his (female) teenage clients as possible, as being 'the kindest way to introduce them to sex'. Although such matters are not usually mentioned in professional literature or on training courses, they do happen. The policy of some managers (Stone, 1988) not to allocate girls who have been sexually abused to male staff, is a clear indication of awareness of these dangers. These managers explain their actions as necessary to protect both the child and the male worker. It seems that the absolute confidentiality of a consultancy or research relationship is the only safe context in which such matters are discussed. But this coyness cannot continue, these problems will have to be acknowledged and ways found to help those at risk. There will always be a measure of risk, but the risks could be minimized and the first step must be to acknowledge the risks.

The following case helps to illustrate some of the problems being discussed. The story concerns a student on a social work course, who during his student placement was convicted for sexually assaulting a number of young boys. It turned out that this person had already served a custodial sentence for a similar offense some years previously; but the college did not discover the details from his curriculum vitae nor did his referees mention anything to do with his previous conviction. Following his arrest, the facts of his earlier conviction came to light, and it became clear why he had resisted the placement, stating that his preference was to work with the elderly and not with children. Under current arrangements this could not happen, or at least is very unlikely to happen. But the really sad thing is that young boys were subjected to abuse by a person who should have been protecting them and this person's life and the chance of a career was ruined for the second time.

What guidance and help is possible in these circumstances? All that is feasible is to appeal to the better side of human nature – if anyone feels themselves to be at risk of abusing children, they must seek a change of job. The children who social workers come into contact with are almost invariably those who have problems of one kind or another; sometimes this may include having been abused. If a person finds themselves in such situations, or feels themselves to be at risk of abusing children, they must seek help or look for other employment. Social workers must raise these matters in a responsible way so that problems are acknowledged and appropriate action, through allocation policies and supervision, expose workers and clients to the minimum risk. At least, it should be possible to start talking about the issue, otherwise it will become the next taboo subject.

Social Class, Gender and Race – the Personal Dimension

There is a personal dimension to all social issues and each professional may experience this in a unique way, depending on their own background and personal values. The class dimension is not often talked about nowadays, it has been replaced by gender and race as central issues. But an analysis of the experiences of any professional group in Britain today, which does not take account of social class, will necessarily be deficient and limited and incomplete. Social work was traditionally a middle class profession, built mainly on the goodwill of middle class women.

It arose from the philanthropic movement of Victorian times and it largely retained this profile well into this century. It was in the 1960s that social work, along with so much else, underwent radical changes. It drew its practitioners from among the students of that time, although not all or even a significant number were 'radical' in any true sense. Many came from working class and lower middle class backgrounds and were motivated to change society, rather than its victims (i.e. the poor and socially deprived clients of 'the welfare'). Social class as a concept was central to their thinking, and they were prepared to challenge and confront assumptions about working class people and life styles and to defend them as they thought necessary.

Another example to illustrate the point. This example deals with a young man of working class origins, who was very happy to be identified as such. He did not allow his socialization into the social work profession to change his accent, his views on working class life or the values he believed to underpin this. Whilst working as a Probation Officer, he challenged a colleague's attempt to, as he saw it, 'stigmatize working class people'; as a result of this episode he eventually left the Probation Service, and has not practiced as a social worker since. The particular incident which had such a dramatic result, was as follows: during a visit to a large working class family, the Probation Officer noticed that people were touching each other quite a lot. Subsequently at a team meeting, when discussing the case, the touching was mentioned and the Probation Officer speculated about the possibility of sexual abuse. This was seen by the young man of working class origin, as an attack on working class culture and family life. He said more or less that if families touching was going to be an indication of abuse, then no working class family would be safe. The subsequent discussion got very heated, and words were exchanged in anger, particularly with respect to middle class people imposing their values and ideas on working class families. The team as a whole rallied around the colleague whose comments had provoked the incident, and the young man was effectively isolated. As a result, his position in the team became untenable and, after some time, he left. He felt himself to be a victim of class prejudice, and that the reason he received no support was because he had actively rejected middle class values, declared himself to be working class, and actively tried to make social workers more aware and accountable in this respect.

It is very unlikely that such issues would arise in such a way today, but social class remains an issue in CPW. It is undoubtedly the case that working class children are significantly over-represented on 'At Risk' registers and amongst the residential child care population. The difference now is that the issues have changed and that class has given way to race as the topical subject of the day.

But race simply subsumes the class issue since most of Britain's black population is working class anyhow. But the racial dimension also brings particular problems to individuals and often sets black workers up in isolated and difficult situations. Racism is alive and present in social work and its impact on individual workers can be very destructive indeed. Unfortunately, workers in this, as in other areas of social work, are not always well placed to identify their own interests. They go along with what appears to be well intentioned ideas only to find themselves isolated and marginalised.

Racism and Sexism: Impact on Individual Workers

Racism is a part of everyday life as is sexism, and its effects are felt at an individual personal level by staff and clients of welfare agencies, as in other organisations. An attempt will be made to identify some of the ways racism and sexism, both together and separately, affect individuals. In earlier sections of this book we have examined serious problems and limitations in the understanding and approach to CPW, and it was argued that these factors have direct consequences on the type and quality of service provided. It is against this background and with this analysis in mind that comments, views and suggestions in relation to the way racism and sexism impact on the individual, are located. Typically, the issues of racism and sexism are isolated, and treated as though they are separate entities which can be dealt with, as it were, in a vacuum.

But let us look at CPW within a context of the development of social work generally and examine the inherent tensions, weaknesses and problems the profession faces in developing a coherent response. This process should in turn provide a context for individuals to understand their own experiences as women, as black people, and as working class people, which helps make sense of these experiences. It has already been observed that social work, as a predominantly female profession, (certainly at the point of contact with the client), has not markedly improved the situation of women in general, and in particular, poor working class women. This must clearly relate to the role and purpose of SSDs and to the values and attitudes of the people who staff social services departments. There may be a sociological dimensions to the gender issue, which would explain some female social worker's punitive attitudes to women and child abuse.

The 'collusive mother/colluding mother' is the archetype of this genre; she has been invented by social workers as a means of blaming women for failing to protect children. This view of women's role in child abuse relies on psychoanalytic explanations of human behaviour and society. The bad/good mother is at the heart of all that is right or wrong with people and with society. 'Cherchez la femme' applies not just to thrillers but to child abuse as well. Social workers, in trying to understand and deal with the inherent sexism which has shaped their current views of women, must re-examine the value base of the attitudes. Racism too reflects the roots of the profession's origins and the way the values and attitudes of the middle classes were imposed on a predominantly working class client group.

Attempts to introduce so-called anti-racist and anti-sexist practices in child care work are mainly individually based, and do not offer an effective mechanism to combat these issues on an organisational level. These efforts are targeted on the individual and their impact, if any, will be limited to the individual. The same observations about the accountability of trainers, apply in this area too. The impression is that a lot of what passes for training actually increases an individual's stress by locating the problem at an individual level, and then leaving the person to feel guilty and inadequate. This is not helpful to anyone. Again, practitioners must be prepared to challenge the assumptions on which such training is based and make demands of the organisations to encourage a response to the issues on other than an individual/personal level.

Examine all the material being used in training, does it display class/race/gender bias?

In terms of the personal dimension – there are differences in the way that gender and race issues impact on different categories. Men, for example, experience a lot of pressure to be 'male protectors' of female colleagues. Men are seen as naturally fulfilling this role and the fact that they may be just as weak and scared as their female colleagues is ignored. Men find it difficult to resist the pressure to take this role, but in going along with it they are reinforcing existing stereotypes, and also increasing their own personal stress level. It would be helpful to confront such issues by way of a seminar type discussion in which such problems could be safely raised and discussed without reference to a particular incident or individual. This would help the team to develop a policy on this and related issues and protect individuals from feeling exploited and put-upon because of their gender. Issues of race and gender raise very strong feelings and have to be dealt with sensitively if they are not to set up strong negative reactions, which ultimately work against everyone.

It is undoubtedly the case that black and so-called ethnic minority workers experience pressures and difficulties associated with their racial and cultural backgrounds. Such workers are seen as representing 'their communities' in a way that their colleagues are not, and they are treated as 'experts' in everything to do with being black or belonging to an ethnic minority. And this 'expertise' is based solely on their membership of a particular racial or cultural group. Individual workers find it very hard to resist these pressures, especially when they themselves may define the problems of black children and families in terms that place special value on the contributions from black professionals. It takes quite a lot of strength of character to resist these pressures, as the story told earlier clearly showed.

In CPW work, black social workers have the same remit as other professionals – to protect children. I attended a seminar on 'Child Sexual Abuse' at the Barbados campus of the University of the West Indies, in spring 1989. The participants were practising social workers and social workers-in-training. The seminar covered familiar ground, the same issues and problems which social workers in Britain are grappling with came up again and again. There was no indication that being black gave them any special insights or skills in this work. In Britain the workforce must represent the community it services and racism and sexism must be confronted. But these issues are often confused and simply add to the problems clients and workers face.

The other side of the racial dimension is the fear and resulting paralysis which this subject is supposed to induce in many white workers. Professor Stevenson suggested that white social workers are so petrified of being labelled racist, that this resulted in a kind of paralysis, in which decisions involving black families are just not made. If this is true, it provides further evidence, if such were needed, of the theory deficit and its implications for practice. Without a theoretical basis on which to build an understanding of racial, cultural and gender issues, the individual is left to fend as best as s/he can. This is not to say that an adequate theoretical base would solve all these problems; it would not, but it would be a start. To expose black children to a higher risk of being abused because of inaction brought about by fear of being called a racist, is probably in effect more racist – certainly as far as the victims are concerned. The thing is to be clear about what the roles of professionals are in relation to child protection and then to provide a service which will achieve these goals for all children.

Balancing the Demands of Self and Others
It is important for social workers to be realistic about what they as individuals can achieve, given the organisational and other constraints which they face.

Several practitioners have found the following areas difficult to cope with:

1) Resisting management pressures 'to hype referrals'.

2) Balancing the demands of competing client groups.

3) Balancing the demands of self and others.

In order to justify the Child Protection referral as the legitimate first priority, there is pressure on social workers to classify referrals in line with set guidelines. Even where the nature of the referral is clear, the front line practitioners often experience what they define as Management pressure to 'hype' the referral. This essentially involves coming to a decision that will make the referral fit certain high risk categories in terms of the definition and classification of child abuse. So workers often feel constrained to be much more definite in their diagnosis than they actually are. This is also linked to the fear of public opinion and the media which both the manager and the supervisors, if different, suffer from and which is shared by the practitioner. Since we have established that the social worker in a SSD is not an independent professional but is exercising delegated authority, they are not well placed to challenge management directly. This means that their main responsibility must lie in informing management about the basis of their beliefs and judgments in any particular case. If the evidence is not conclusive it is then the responsibility of management to decide how to classify the case in terms of resource allocation etc.

At the same time, the social worker has a perspective on the case and a professional view as to how it should be classified. But these different factors combine to effectively marginalise the workers perceptions and contributions. There are no easy answers to this or any of the problems we have been considering. Social workers can only work within the existing system, accept their responsibilities, as far as they go, and try to influence management decision making in terms of more professional client-related criteria. There is really not a lot of choice as things stand.

The fact is that many social services departments are currently facing problems in recruiting and retaining staff. This is especially true of London and the South East region. The changing profile of SSDs, with child protection and other statutory work constituting a significant part of its activities, means that people who do not want to do such work decide to work in the voluntary sector or related agencies. So staff shortages in the SSDs are linked to several factors and are likely to persist. At the same time, the demand for services continues to expand. In theory SSDs remain generic in their approach, which means that, in theory at least, practitioners should be working with a variety of client groups. In practice, because of some of the reasons discussed earlier, CPW dominates the SSDs work profile.

This places individual social workers in extremely difficult situations: a practitioner may have planned a support programme for, say, a young person leaving care. This would involve a series of meetings and perhaps training activities with the young person. As the programme gets underway a CP referral comes up. There is no way that the practitioner has the discretion to decide how to deal with that situation. It does not matter who has the greater need for attention the procedures are clear and must be followed. This together with the media phobia, which often determines how people react, ensures that whatever the personal or professional judgement of the individual worker as to the urgency of each piece of work, s/he has to deal with the CP referral as the priority. One result of this is to leave the worker feeling worried and guilty about the person s/he has abandoned, and the work s/he has left 'hanging'. It seems that this again puts an unfair burden on the individual worker, who has been constrained by law, procedures and management to act in a given way. Social workers should educate clients, especially young people who will be the voters and taxpayers of the future about the realities facing SSDs. They should explain the possibility of having to abandon a piece of work, not in terms of their own individual responsibility, since it isn't, but as the result of legislation and policies which determine what they can do.

It is likely that some social workers will see this as off-loading these problems onto clients and will reject it as 'passing the buck'. But, as things stand, they are blamed by clients and other colleagues for being unreliable and failing to keep to agreements. If some attempt were made to educate and inform the public about these choices (or lack of them), it would at least help to put what is happening in a proper context. Each worker can only do his or her best, after that, it is necessary to locate the responsibility for the quality of service where it really belongs. Do not make unrealistic demands on yourself, do not take on personal responsibility for the inadequacies of your department. Acknowledge these and work for improvements, but accept that in the meantime things will continue to be far from perfect.

Social workers often find it difficult to say 'no' to the demands made on them, even when they are clearly unable to meet such demands. This tendency has to be combatted, in the interest of all concerned; it is better to avoid the build-up of problems, by saying 'no' at the onset. Colleagues are usually very understanding if the reasons for the refusal to help are given. It is not the saying 'no', it is the way it is done. But, even so, if care is taken and reactions are still negative, that has to be accepted as the price to be paid for being firm about how much you can realistically do. In the long term, this is far better than trying to please everyone and becoming over-stretched, over-tired and consequently failing to perform adequately at any level of the job.

Stress in Child Protection Work
The last section looked briefly at some of the problems concerned with being realistic about the demands on self and others. This leads

us very naturally onto stress and its effects on workers in this field. The first thing to say is that one persons 'stress' is another persons 'stimulation'. But most would agree that CPW is very stressful. Many of the reasons for this will be clear from much that has already been said and some of the suggestions which have been made will, if successfully employed, help to modify the conditions which promote stress.

As far as responses and coping mechanisms are concerned, what is most important is for each person to know exactly what it is about particular situations/problems which makes the associated stresses unbearable. This can only come from individual analysis; paralleling this, there must be an analysis of situations which are challenging but not stressful. Why? What makes one stressful and the other challenging? It can be very helpful for practitioners to analyse their own work to see how they function in terms of stress management.

It is important for each individual to try to identify the precise way stress actually affects them, linking this to personal and professional dimensions in terms of effects. It is also important to feedback to others their contribution to the general stress levels in the Department/Team/Office and the way this impacts on morale and performance. Some of the stresses associated with CPW are an inevitable part of the work. Feeling empathy with the pain of the victims is a natural human feeling which should not be denied. Beyond that comes the continuing need to offer a better, more effective child protection service to the next generation of children, and to hope that there will be a diminishing need for such services, one day. In terms of stress management it is hoped that the strategies and ideas presented in this book, together with the insights and understandings the text has tried to promote, will encourage child protection workers to a point where they can work effectively, using the strengths of the existing system, and their own professional skills, to try to provide children with the best service that the profession is capable of giving.

Job Satisfaction in Child Protection Work

The best way to begin to achieve a degree of job satisfaction in CPW is for each person to identify what constitutes job satisfaction and work towards this. The usual indicators of job satisfaction may not apply in this context, in that success may have very little meaning when you're at the sharp end of human suffering and debauchery. But although the end product of the work may not be 'satisfying' in any conventional sense, it must always be a source of satisfaction and professional pride to have performed well and competently in very demanding and challenging situations. Ultimately it is a job of work which is being discussed, and performance and job satisfaction must be judged against what people normally expect from a job.

Summary of the Main Points
This chapter looked at the personal dimension to CPW, analysing the work in terms of its impact on professionals as persons and focusing on:

1) Social workers as parents, survivors, or offenders.

2) Issues of class, gender and race examining these for their impact on individuals, as males, females, black and white people.

3) The class origin of the social work profession was discussed in relation to the class background and values of the profession.

4) The need to achieve a balance between competing demands – in terms of personal expectations and the demands of others – was identified and discussed.

5) The stressful nature of CPW was discussed, and ways of coping with this stress were suggested.

6) Social workers were encouraged not to take personal responsibility for the limitations of the child protection service. But to acknowledge these, and do the best they can.

7) The difficulty of applying the conventional understanding of 'job satisfaction' in this context was acknowledged.

Chapter 6
Concluding Remarks

In his introduction to the review of *Research and Innovation in Child Abuse and Neglect*, (1982) the editor Leavitt, commented that:

> 'Throughout the history of the world children have been abused and neglected in every possible way: physical neglect, sexual abuse, and psychological abuse/neglect. Today, if there is any change in the situation it is worse.'

Things have not improved since 1982, referral figures for child abuse cases continue to rise; but these figures are not a reliable guide since they generally exclude abuse in boarding schools and residential establishments. Society continues to undergo massive changes, and the role and composition of the family are at the heart of these changes (Bradshaw, 1980; The General Household Survey, 1989). Like it or not these changes have resulted in the State expanding its role in child protection, and social workers are charged with the responsibility of providing this child protection service. But social workers have to tread a very thin line between respect for the rights of the child; respect for the sanctity of family life; and respect for the rights of fellow citizens suspected of child abuse. Social workers also have to implement the law and carry out their professional duties.

Very often these activities are not compatible so how are they to decide which one to pursue? Sometimes they make the wrong judgment and when this happens the social workers themselves are attacked and vilified. The development of 'a siege mentality' is not a positive response – this helps neither the professionals nor the potential victims – what is required is a response which will enable social workers to exert more influence in the workplace, so that they do not have to continue to tolerate inadequate management and supervision, only to be blamed themselves when things go wrong.

Social workers encounter many hazards and difficulties in undertaking CPW, threats of violence to themselves and their children, sometimes they experience actual violence. The nature of the work itself takes its toll on people's emotional and psychological health. The training they get is often inadequate, and the methods used are sometimes questionable adding to the stress of an already stressful job. How do practitioners cope? How do they 'survive' the stresses of CPW?

Many do not cope very well at all, they simply plod along doing their best to 'cover themselves' and to avoid being the subject of the next tabloid newspaper attack. This book tries to provide a more positive response to some of the problems associated with CPW. It does this by analysing child abuse and CPW; by looking at the major issues which impact on the practice of CPW; examining some of the common problems and difficulties experienced by social workers; giving hints, and suggesting coping strategies.

The social issues of class, race and gender were examined for their impact on practice. As was the abuse of children in residential care and the fact that professionals may be victims or perpetrators of abuse. It's still not possible to make an omelette without breaking eggs – the credibility of the profession and the protection of children requires that these problems be raised and openly discussed. This book provides practitioners with the means to begin that process in their own small way. Neither social work in general, nor child protection work in particular is 'an impossible task', (Gibson, 1989); the problem is in having an accurate view of what that task consists of. Practitioners have been provided with a view of CPW, it is a tool for them to use as they wish.

A social worker after reading the first draft of this book agreed with its general message, but felt that it was making too heavy demands on practitioners. But if social workers don't do something who will? Ask yourself – If not you, who? If not now? When? Let the reply be a positive one. And good luck.

References

Association of Directors of Social Services: 1989a Survey of Child Abuse Referrals.
1989b Briefing Note, No 9.
1989c Workforce Survey.

Barclay Report (1982) Social Workers – Their Roles and Tasks. NISW. Bedford Square Press.

BASW (1985) The Management of Child Abuse. British Association of Social Workers.

Behlemer G K (1982) Child Abuse and Moral Reform in England 1870 – 1908. Standford U Press.

Bowlby J (1953) Child Care and the Growth of Love, Penguin.

Bradshaw (1980) Family Life Today, in Public Policy and Family Life, Policy Studies Institute.

Brunel University Institute of Organisational Studies (1974). Social Services Departments – Developing Patterns of Work and Organisation. Heinemann.

Butler-Sloss Lord Justice (1989) Appeal Court Ruling. London.

Butrym (1976) The Nature of Social Work. Macmillan.

Children's Legal Centre (1988) Child Abuse Procedure – The Child's Viewpoint. The Children's Legal Centre.

Children's Society (1989) Homeless and Hungry. CS London.

Community Care – various as referenced in the text.

Cooper C L and Bowles D (1977) 'Hurt or Helped'? A Survey of Sensitivity Training for Managers. Training Services Agency.

Corby (1988) Study of Social Work in Child Abuse Cases. University of Liverpool.

Corby and Mills (1986) Child Abuse Risks and Responses. *British Journal of Social Work*, 16, 5.

Dale R *et al* (eds) (1981) Politics, Partiarchy and Practice. Falmer Press/OUP

Department of Health and Social Security (Now Department of Health).
1982 A Study of Inquiry Reports. HMSO.
1986 Child Abuse Working Together for the Protection of Children. Draft Circular. HMSO.

Dingwall *et al* (1983) The Protection of Children – State Intervention and Family Life. Basil Blackwell.

Doyle C (1986) Management Sensitivity – An Issue in Child Sexual Abuse Training. *Child Abuse Review*.

Fairtlough (1983) Responsibility for Incest – a Feminist View. University of East Anglia.

Fielding *et al* (1988) Interim Report: The Surrey Constabulary/Surrey

Social Services Joint Investigation Initiative in Cases of Child Sexual Abuse. Surrey University.

Gelles R and Cornell C (1985) Intimate Violence in Families. Sage.

General Household Survey (1989) Preliminary Report. OPCS 89/1.

Gibson D (1989) Social Work – The Impossible Task? Paper to the International Association of Schools of Social Work Seminar, (ERG) Bled, Yugoslavia. Teesside Polytechnic.

Gillner H and Morris A (1981) Care and Discretion – Social Workers. Decisions with Delinquents. Burnett Books.

Girma-Asrat (1988) Afro-Caribbean Children in Day Care. Unpublished, Surrey University.

Goldberg M (1979) Ends and Means in Social Work. NISW.

Hadley R and McGarth (eds) (1981) Going Local – Neighbourhood Social Services. Bedford Square Press.

Horncastle P and Bull R (1985) Human Awareness Training For Police Recruits – An Evaluation. NELP.

ISPCAN (1989) Invitation Programme for the 8th International Congress 'Child Abuse or Child Protection – Society's Dilemma'. Hamburg, Germany.

Inquiry Reports:

1974 – Report of the Committee of Inquiry into the Care and Supervision provided in relation to Maria Caldwell. HMSO.

1986 – A Child In Trust: Report of the Panel of Inquiry into the Circumstances Surrounding the death of Jasmine Beckford. London Borough of Brent.

1989 – The Doreen Mason Report. The Borough Borough of Lewisham.

1984 – Report of The Committee of On Sexual Offenses against Children (The Badgley Report). Ministry of Justice, Ottawa Canada.

1987 – Report of the Inquiry into Child Abuse in Cleveland 1987 CM 412 HMSO.

Jaffe S and Scherl D J (1969) Acute Psychosis precipitated by T-Group Experiences. *Archives of General Psychiatry*, 21.

Kempe H *et al* (1962) The Battered Child Syndrome. *Journal of American Medical Association*, 181.

Kielsler S (1973) Emotions in Groups. *Journal of Humanistic Psychology*, 13,3.

Lankin M (1969) Some Ethical Issues in Sensitivity Training. *American Psychologist*, 24.

Leavitt (ed) (1982) Research and Innovation in Child Abuse and Neglect. NATO.

Legislation and Social Work Practice. Commission on The Family, Occasional Paper No, 11.

Local Government Training Board (1987) The Development of Senior Managers in Social Services Departments. LGTB, Luton.

MacIntosh M (1988) The Family, Regulation and The Public Sphere. Open University.

MacIver R M and Page C H (1950) Society an Introductory Analysis. Macmillan.

MacLeod V (1982) Whose Child? The Family in Child Care

MacLeod M and Saraga E (1988) Challenging The Orthodoxy. *Feminist Review*, Vol. 28.

Mass M (1989) The Need For a Paradigm Shift in Social Work: The Study of Parenting. (ERG Seminar Paper.) Hebrew University, Jerusalem.

Millham (1981) 'Children in Trouble'. A paper presented to the All-Party Parliament Group for Children. Dartington Social Research Unit.

Moore J (1985) The ABC of Child Abuse Work. Methuen.

Morrison T (1981) 'Tar Baby'. Grafton Books.

National Society for the Protection of Children: (1988) Treatment Approaches to Child Sexual Abuse.
(1989) Annual Statistics. NSCCP HQ.

Newman C (1989) Young Runaways . . . . findings from Britain's first safe house. Children's Society.

Newspapers – As referenced in the text.

Perry L (1983) Independent Representation for Children in Neglect and Abuse Cases in Leavitt op cited. NATO.

Rowan C (1982) 'Motherhood and The Early Welfare State, 1900–1920'. Critical Social Policy.

Sheppherd M (1982) Perceptions of Child Abuse: A Critique of Individualism. University of East Anglia.

Smith P B (1975) Are there adverse effects of Sensitivity Training? *Journal of Humanistic Psychology*, 15.

Social Services Inspectorate (Department of Health):
1986 – Inspection of the Supervision of social workers in the assessment and monitoring of child abuse when children, subject to a care order have been returned home. SSI.
1989 – Report on Inspection of Child Abuse Services in Cumbria SSD. SSI

Stevenson O (1988) Keynote address to the NSPCC Conference. Unpublished, Nottingham University.

Stone M (1988) Social Work Training For Child Protection Work. University of Surrey.
(1989) Young People Leaving Care – Research Report. Royal Philanthropic Society.

Westminster City Council (1987) Evaluation Project Report. (Westminster Report) WCC.

Woodroofe (1974) From Charity to Social Work. Routledge and Kegan Paul.

Yalom 1 D and Leiberman M I (1971 'A Study Of Encounter Casualties'. *Archives of General Psychiatry*, 25.

Index